FROM BOARDBOOK
TO FACEBOOK

FROM BOARDBOOK TO FACEBOOK

Children's Services in an Interactive Age

ADELE M. FASICK

 LIBRARIES UNLIMITED

AN IMPRINT OF ABC-CLIO, LLC
Santa Barbara, California • Denver, Colorado • Oxford, England

Library of Congress Cataloging-in-Publication Data

Fasick, Adele M.
    From boardbook to Facebook : children's services in an interactive age / Adele M. Fasick.
        p. cm.
    Includes bibliographical references and index.
    ISBN 978-1-59884-468-9 (hardcopy : alk. paper) — ISBN 978-1-59884-469-6 (ebook) 1. Children's libraries—United States. 2. Interactive multimedia—United States. I. Title.
    Z718.2.U6F368 2011
    027.62'5—dc22   2011010142

ISBN: 978-1-59884-468-9
EISBN: 978-1-59884-469-6

15 14 13 12 11   1 2 3 4 5

This book is also available on the World Wide Web as an eBook.
Visit www.abc-clio.com for details.

Libraries Unlimited
An Imprint of ABC-CLIO, LLC

ABC-CLIO, LLC
130 Cremona Drive, P.O. Box 1911
Santa Barbara, California 93116-1911

This book is printed on acid-free paper ∞

Manufactured in the United States of America

CONTENTS

PREFACE

Tomorrow is our permanent address.

—e. e. cummings

Children born in the 21st century are living in a constantly changing world of media. We have heard a great deal about the "information revolution" that has dramatically shifted the way information and entertainment are produced, communicated, and used. The development of computers has made it possible to amass large quantities of data and to store it in text or video format for retrieval by individuals or groups locally or at a distance. This has changed the way people earn their livings, do business, and entertain themselves. For the average person, however, and especially for children, the change has been evolutionary rather than revolutionary. Many libraries and schools provide collections and services that are not dramatically different from the ones they were providing 20 years ago with only slight adjustments toward more efficient catalogs and acquisition processes.

This book is organized in sections to look at children and the services libraries provide to them. After a general overview of the way media for children have changed in the last 10 years, section I, "Changes in Children's Lives" examines the lives of different age groups of children in our communities. Whether they are preschoolers, school-age children, or so-called tweens, their worlds are far different from the worlds of their parents and older generations. Much of their knowledge of the world and their interactions with it are shaped by electronic media of all kinds. We examine the types of services and programs that have been offered by libraries in the past and the extent to which they are being modified to take advantage of the different experiences of today's children.

Section II, "Literacies for the 21st Century," considers evolving notions of literacy and how the demands of our global civilization have spurred efforts to promote universal literacy. Because of the increasing mobility of individuals and groups, the state of literacy throughout the world has implications for libraries in developed countries where literacy rates are high. A library in America may serve the children of Somali subsistence farmers as well as those of internet entrepreneurs. Collections and services should be designed to serve children of many varied backgrounds.

Information literacy is one of the most important of the many literacies today's children must understand. A chapter on information literacy examines how reference services can be provided through different media and delivery tools to children in the library, at home, or in other locations.

New media and new types of services require changes in library buildings, so the "Buildings for the Future" section concentrates on how physical spaces influence services and collections. Many library buildings still in use today were planned and built several generations ago, and this book examines some of the assumptions that dictated the planning and design of these older libraries. The changing patterns of media use require changes in our views of what a library should be and what we expect of the buildings that house libraries. Libraries are no longer restricted to a building; they can send their services out to the community, although usually a library building remains the hub of those services.

Several possible models for library services to children are examined. These range from traditional book-centered collections enhanced by some technological advances to various patterns of online and brick-and-mortar information services. We propose the possibility of building a blended library that uses the best of past practice and welcomes the new features of advanced technology. Although libraries must continue to provide the basic resources for reading and understanding information, new methods and possibilities are opening for all of us. Library collections are evolving from print materials to interactive resources that children contribute to as well as use. Constant change is the only constant. Librarians can look forward to offering the best possible services to children who will be living in a world none of us can predict.

Being a children's librarian in a world of constant change is not easy, and the final section of the book, "Preparing to Meet the Future," deals with facilitating change in the library and reaching out to the community to ensure that people understand and accept the changes. Although library and information schools have been at the forefront of university programs offering online formats and introducing new technology into the classroom, there is no time to rest on our laurels. Librarians will have to remain open to change. Now and in the future, children's librarians must accept the notion of education and training as ongoing processes as they adapt to a swiftly changing profession. As e. e. cummings once wrote, "tomorrow is our permanent address." That is true of children who look to the future with excitement, and it is also true of the adults who serve them. Welcoming the future may sometimes be a challenge, but it is also an inspiration for a profession that has always built on hope, not fear.

1

———◆·◆———

CHILDREN'S SERVICES MOVING INTO THE FUTURE

The sight of a preteen nimbly tapping out a text message with one hand at the same time that she combs her hair and peers at herself in the mirror is unnerving to some adults. What has happened to the childhood we knew? Talking endlessly on the phone has been a ritual for American young people for generations, but what about phones that are not used for talking but for texting? Silent messaging can't be much fun.

Librarians, like most parents of today's children, grew up in the 20th century, when Beverly Cleary showed us a different view of childhood. In those days when Ramona Quimby worried about losing her best friend or impressing her kindergarten teacher, childhood appeared relatively peaceful and secluded from the world. Today's child grows up with a constant barrage of media telling stories of battling families and bizarre behavior that used to be hidden from children. Music pulsates through their lives from the ear buds of their iPods, which deliver rhythms from far-off countries and language seldom heard in mainstream media. How do we serve these children? Do libraries still matter? To answer those questions, we have to look back and think about history.

ARE LIBRARIES FOR CHILDREN STILL IMPORTANT?

Children's libraries were introduced during a time of information and recreational scarcity. They flourished during the early 20th century, when print was almost the only means of telling stories or conveying information at a distance. Public schools were still a relatively new institution, and most children finished their schooling with eighth grade. High school was for the elite, and colleges were only a dream in most communities. The public library gave the general population a means of continuing their education by providing access to books.

It's difficult for people today to realize how little print material was available a century ago. Most communities had newspapers, but except in the large cities, newspapers covered a small range of local news, with only occasional articles about national or international events. Middle-class families could purchase magazines, but most of these were too expensive for working-class families. The majority of children had little access to books, yet books were for most families the most available source of both stories and information about the world. Few families owned more than a handful of books; many owned none at all. Bookstores were rare except in a few large cities and were available mostly to financially privileged families. Children's services in public libraries and later school libraries were developed in most communities to offer children access to books they wanted for school and for entertainment.

The library buildings and facilities of the pre–World War II era give an indication of the role they were expected to play. As a British historian of libraries notes (Black and Rankin 2009, p. 4), the children's sections in early libraries give a feeling of the schoolroom. The typical arrangement of the room featured rectangular tables flanked by straight-backed chairs. The underlying message conveyed by the libraries was that they were a shelter from the outside world and a place where serious young people were expected to behave themselves and appreciate the benefits they were given.

As time went by, children's libraries became less austere, reflecting the philosophy that reading should be pleasurable and libraries should offer children a chance to enjoy beauty in many forms. Anne Carroll Moore, who pioneered children's services at the New York Public Library, had as her goal providing inviting spaces where children could read and borrow books while being supervised by librarians who appreciated and understood both children and books.

Library design and collections reflected the changing social expectations for educational experiences. Libraries became more informal and homelike, with colorful posters and cozy storytime areas provided. The age of the child audience dropped, and children were no longer expected to be able to read before they started using the library. Welcoming preschoolers naturally led to welcoming their parents and caregivers, and librarians became role models in demonstrating how to encourage reading and the use of books. Still, throughout the first half of the 20th century, the emphasis was strongly on books and reading as the focus of library work. In most communities, there was still an acute shortage of reading materials for young people, and libraries were the major source of supply. The postwar years led to an explosion of paperback book publishing, and eventually, libraries found themselves competing with bookstores, discount stores, and school book fairs as the major supplier of reading material.

Throughout these years, children and adults became less dependent on books for entertainment. Radio and later television were introduced into homes, and by the 1990s, more than 90 percent of Americans had access to least one television set at home. Television became the major supplier of entertainment for both adults and children, and when videotapes made an appearance, the trend accelerated. With VCRs in the home, families could buy or rent inexpensive videos for their children or tape television programs for later replaying. The majority of American children no longer needed books to supply exciting narrative entertainment.

Even though the entertainment media migrated from print to visual formats, books were acknowledged to be the most important source of information for both adults and children. Schools relied on textbooks supplemented by an increasing supply of attractive nonfiction books published by both trade and educational publishers. Some parents bought atlases, encyclopedias, and dictionaries so that their children would have reference sources at home, and libraries offered these resources to children to supplement whatever their home offered. Libraries played an important role in supplying resources to equalize information access for families at all economic levels.

As the 20th century gave way to the 21st, the world went through a revolution in the ways both recreation and information were made available.

- Picture books were turned into filmstrips and then into videos and DVDs.
- Narrative books gave way to films and then to videos and other digitized formats.
- Recordings went to cassettes, CDs, and downloadable formats.
- Atlases gave way to Google Maps or other formats.
- Dictionaries went online and provided auditory as well as visual information about words.
- Encyclopedias were digitized and incorporated pictures, videos, audio clips, and other formats.
- Children's periodicals began to decrease in numbers.
- Current event and newspaper files became videos and podcasts.
- Reference services tended to fade as more users posed questions online.
- Online repositories of videos and images, such as YouTube and Flickr, replaced both print and digital resources stored in libraries.
- Study carrels became redundant as children worked in computer-focused groups rather than individually with print sources.
- Separate collections for children became more open as age barriers to all formats dropped. Children and their parents watched the same entertainment sources.

What Do Libraries as Institutions Offer to Children?

Even though children and their media have changed, some things remain constant. The children coming into our libraries vary greatly in age and background. They may have been raised in a trailer park at the end of an unpaved rural road or in a McMansion in the fanciest part of town. Their parents may be homeless drifters, teenage high school dropouts, respected doctors, or wealthy factory owners. No matter how different the children and how changed the media they prefer, libraries still have a mandate to provide collections and services for all.

The library as a public institution offers well-defined services for all children. There are some things all children need to find when they use a library, no matter what kind of family the come from:

- Security in a safe environment
- A chance to try out their skills and find out what they can do
- Opportunities to interact with other children and develop social skills
- Access to recreational formats, especially books, that are not available elsewhere
- Access to information and knowledge at a level they can understand
- Tools to help them hone their skills and manipulate the information they are learning

Most librarians would accept these needs as legitimate, and they try to provide resources to meet them, but as society changes, librarians must ensure that their collections and services are still the ones that best meet children's needs.

In September 2009, the headmaster of a prep school in Massachusetts caused a furor by announcing that the school would give away all of the books in its library collection in order to focus on electronic resources. In a 2009 article in the *Boston Globe*, James Tracy is quoted as saying, "When I look at books, I see an outdated technology, like scrolls before books. . . . Instead of a traditional library with 20,000 books, we're building a virtual library where students will have access to millions of books" (Abel 2009). Many librarians reacted with scathing denunciations of even considering the possibility of a library without books, yet if we accept the basic function of libraries as providing information and recreation, surely all formats must be examined for their continuing relevance. One speaker at the 2009 IFLA conference took the following position:

> I shall argue that public libraries need to move away from defining themselves in relation to their holdings, their products, towards defining themselves in relation to particular functions for users. These functions are to do with facilitating quality of knowledge in relation to information, entertainment and communication. (Drotner 2009, p. 1)

More than ever, libraries must consider themselves as a part of society serving particular social needs, defining themselves by the services they offer rather than by their collections. As the structure of information dissemination in society changes, so must the role of libraries. Because children's librarians serve a group that by its nature embraces the new rather than looking back at the past, children's librarians should be in the forefront of designing forward-looking services.

What Do Library Services Offer to Children?

Most members of the public still think of libraries as sources of books and as places frequented by people who like to read or those who have to read for school or professional purposes. Certainly, libraries were started to give access to books, but have the basic purposes of libraries changed now that the media landscape is so different? Is reading still an important skill that needs the encouragement of an institutional framework? These are important questions to ask ourselves.

Importance of Reading to Young Children

Learning to read is one of the crucial experiences for young children in our society. As one writer expresses it,

> We were never born to read. Human beings invented reading only a few thousand years ago. And with this invention, we rearranged the very organization of our brain, which in turn expanded the ways we were able to think. . . . Reading is one of the single most remarkable inventions in history; the ability to record history is one of the consequences. (Wolf 2007, p. 3)

Children who are given no education at all learn to talk and understand language, and they can interpret pictures and visual symbols, but they do not learn to read without help from others. Getting information from a text is far different from getting it by listening to words or looking at pictures. Reading requires the brain to establish different pathways to understanding. We are only beginning to understand why literacy makes such a difference to individuals and societies as scientists learn more about how the human brain works.

Long before cognitive scientists began to study the reading process, librarians came up with their own strategies to encourage reading. Many parents and teachers knew from observation that children love being read to, and fortunately, reading to children is pleasurable for adults too, so reading aloud became a common activity. Many parents, for various reasons, do not read to their young children, and this often makes a significant difference in how well the child does in school. Family reading is an ideal setting for a child's first reading experience: "How a child first learns to read is a tale of either magic and fairies or missed chances and unnecessary loss" (Wolf 2007, p. 82).

Early children's librarians established the tradition of having storyhours in the library, and that practice has continued to this day. This tradition has been validated by its success in encouraging children to read, but its effect has never reached all children in a community. Now the importance of reading is being challenged by the existence of other media, although reading is championed by a wide range of voices. The critic Harold Bloom wrote, "Reading well makes children more interesting both to themselves and others, a process in which they will develop a sense of being separate and distinct selves" (2001, p. 20). More statistically minded researchers have pointed out the relationship between not learning to read well during the early school years and later delinquency (Hogenson 1974). There is much dispute about whether low reading abilities and delinquency are causally related, but almost everyone agrees that children who learn to read successfully while young do better in later life.

We know some of the practical means by which we can help young children move into reading because we know some of the factors that help a child become a reader:

- Learning spoken language by interacting with parents and other adults
- Being read to frequently, preferably by a beloved adult
- Seeing books and having access to them

Although librarians cannot replicate or take the place of the home environment of every child, they can, and do, offer supplementary programs that help fill the gap.

Services Offered by Most Libraries

For the most part, children's libraries are still offering fairly traditional services to children. Almost all public libraries offer a range of materials and services:

- Storyhours for preschoolers
- A carefully chosen collection of resources designed for children from birth through the elementary school grades
- Summer reading programs
- Reference service in the library

- Readers' advisory services
- Special programs such as author or illustrator visits

Many libraries find their collections and programs very successful and are satisfied to be serving the needs of a large segment of the population; however, others believe that not all children are being served and that the library is in danger of becoming irrelevant to a large segment of the population. Who is right? It's impossible to answer that question. In these times of limited resources, libraries are congratulating themselves on being able to carry on as well as they can. Reading rooms are becoming more crowded as people cut back on expenses. Some summer reading programs have grown because fewer children are going to camp. Storyhour programs are crowded, and unemployed parents are taking children to the library in an effort to find affordable activities for them.

Yet there is a nagging sense of doubt because media sources keep telling us that children are "digital natives," more at home online than in the world of books, and many people believe public libraries will be unnecessary when broadband access becomes available to all families. What can librarians do to keep up with the changing world of childhood yet at the same time hold onto the values developed over years of library education?

HOW DO TODAY'S CHILDREN INTERACT WITH MEDIA?

First, we need to look at the situation as it exists in the United States today—or as close to today as we can get. One truth we should acknowledge at the outset is that every statistic we find about media use represents only one point in time. The numbers are changing from month to month as well as from year to year. There are few classics in the digital world, only an endless stream of information coming in, being processed, arousing attention, and then passing on into history, often before half the population has realized it existed.

A Kaiser Family Foundation study in 2003 (in the far-distant past by electronic media standards) found that in a typical day,

- 83 percent of children up to age six had interacted with one or another form of electronic media, and
- 79 percent had read or been read to during the day (Rideout et al. 2003, p. 4).

However, the time spent with electronic media paints a different picture. Most children on a typical day spent

- 2 hours or more in front of a television or computer screen and
- 40 minutes or less reading or being read to.

Two-thirds of the children studied live in homes where the television is on half of the time or more, even if no one is watching. Clearly, children are growing up in a world saturated by media.

More statistics are available on television viewing than on the use of other electronic media, but a recent study in Australia (Zevenbergen and Logan 2008) fo-

Children's activities (N = 45)	Total %
Games, noneducational	59.9
Games, educational	79.5
Drawing	48.9
Software packages	15.5
Prewriting activities	20.7
Modeling (copying behavior)	15.7
Internet	39.8
Free play	26.2

Figure 1.1 Computer activities by preschool children. Data from Zevenbergen and Logan (2008).

cused on the ways in which preschool children use computers. Although this study was small and cannot be generalized, it is still surprising to discover how many children interact with computers before they even reach school age. They use computers for several types of activities, both educational and recreational.

The experiences preschoolers have with computers are likely to affect their use of libraries. These children who grow up playing computer games and checking information online grow into the middle schoolers who find it more natural to communicate by texting and to find information through Twitter. Yet comparatively few libraries take advantage of this knowledge of the online world when they purchase materials or plan services. Why should this be? There are many possible barriers.

Barriers to Libraries' Use of Modern Technologies for Children

1. **Large differences among children in the amount of computer use.** In a library setting, many children head straight for the public computers. Staff must handle a number of questions about computer use and give instructions. They become aware of the needs of these children and may not notice other children who are quietly handling their own computer usage without the intervention of any adult. This may lead staff members to underestimate the desire for newer formats and services among their patrons as a whole. Children who do not have access to computers at home, however, may also be missing access to mobile phones and social media, which are becoming an increasingly important part of socialization for tweens and teens. A lack of patron demand for a service or materials does not necessarily mean that the need does not exist. It may just be that patrons don't know what could be provided for them.

2. **Generational differences in library staff.** Librarians were among the first professionals to use computers in their work, but many children's librarians concentrated more on learning about books than on learning about

computers or technology. Older librarians may shy away from demonstrating their less-than-perfect understanding of text messaging or YouTube in front of their patrons. This reluctance is often increased by stereotypical media presentations of inept adults unable to handle new media as well as young people.

3. **Reluctance to spend money on untested methods and tools.** Librarianship is a conservative profession. Much of the work done in libraries is designed to preserve resources that might otherwise be lost. This leads librarians to value long-lasting books rather than the more ephemeral electronic formats. Over the years, many libraries have refused to accept new formats, and some libraries that did buy new formats have regretted some of their purchases. Many audiovisual and electronic formats have come and gone; libraries have been caught with shelves full of unwanted filmstrips, 16mm films, vinyl recordings, and audio cassettes. Now DVDs, which have been a popular part of library collections for several years, appear to be on their way out. Librarians worry about spending public funds on laptops or ebook readers that may be supplanted by other formats requiring yet another round of spending. This concern makes good sense, and the value of spending on new formats must constantly be questioned and tested.

4. **Fear of possible damage from new media.** Many adults are uncomfortable with change, especially if it affects their children and the relationships between children and parents. Teachers and librarians are especially vulnerable to criticism if they offer young people materials and services their parents find unfamiliar. Back in the 1950s, when comic books had a resurgence, there was an outcry about how dangerous they were to children. *Seduction of the Innocent*, written by psychiatrist Frederic Wertham, was influential and inspired congressional hearings about the dangers of reading comic books. Librarians, on the whole, agreed with these concerns and did not stock comics in libraries. Early reactions to children's use of the internet were similar. Many journal articles focused almost exclusively on the possible dangers to children of unsupervised internet use. Congressional hearings were held, and the result was the Children's Internet Protection Act (CIPA) passed in 2000. Many libraries have welcomed filtering software and use it to limit children's access to inappropriate online material. Arguments can be made about the extent to which children need to be protected, but it's unfortunate that the emphasis on possible bad effects of internet use have shadowed the introduction of electronic media into libraries. Only gradually did librarians turn their attention to the value that the internet could add to library resources. As more and different digital media become available, it would be unfortunate to allow fear of possible evil to prevent libraries from embracing the value they might bring.

5. **Lack of awareness of the possible functions of interactive media of many kinds.** Library staff members are not always the first in a community to adopt new methods of information gathering or entertainment. Over the years, librarians have learned about the value of books as sources of information and recreation, and some believe that other sources are not needed or are inferior. The number of individuals who successfully access and use these other sources for recreation and information makes this belief

questionable. The need for library services cannot be judged only by the satisfaction of people who use the library.

6. **A belief that only by bringing people into the library can service be provided.** Most public and school libraries use technology to help individuals access various library services without coming to the library. According to a 2008 survey published in *Public Libraries* (Varvel and Lei 2009), 98 percent of public libraries have websites; 83.5 percent have pages devoted to children and young adult services. Still, the goal of many of these websites is to encourage patrons to come to the library building. Catalogs are available online, and often databases can be accessed, but far fewer provide reference service at a distance:

- 60 percent offer email or web form reference.
- 40 percent offer chat reference.
- 18 percent provide reference via instant messaging.

For most librarians, it appears that the "real" library is the brick-and-mortar building.

7. **A belief that books are the only legitimate form of reading.** Books have been legitimized as the appropriate way for a child to read. Literacy campaigns and summer reading programs concentrate on encouraging children to read more and more books. Unfortunately, this sometimes seems a losing battle because reading books for pleasure appears to be declining, at least according to some reports. Certainly, reading has changed. Many adults and students do as much reading from a screen as they do from a page. Some researchers have pointed out that these changes in reading habits do not mean the end of literacy, but rather changes in format. This is an important factor and librarians should consider its implications. One researcher puts it this way:

> Perhaps reading as we have traditionally defined it is at risk. It seems that an expanded definition of reading should be developed that encourages a balance between narrative and exposition; hard copy and electronic media. While there may be a decline in the reading of literary books, the *Reading at Risk* survey has not convinced me that there is a decline in overall reading. (Gambrell 2005, p. 590)

These factors may help to explain why children's libraries have not changed as quickly as children's lives have. There are other reasons, of course, among them the constant pressure of budget constraints that hinder innovation in most public institutions. Many changes require an investment of money and time for planning. The digital media that increasingly dominate our world have been built on a model of private enterprise with market demand driving new production. This has tended to weaken support for many public institutions. Some critics suggest that profit-making groups are more efficient and should be allowed to run public schools and public libraries. The traditional methods of financing public libraries through tax funds have been sorely tested by recent economic downturns. It is no surprise that librarians choose to stick to traditional services that many board members prefer, rather than attempting radical changes that might appeal to young users. Nonetheless, it is obvious that many librarians are dissatisfied with the way things are. Much good work is being accomplished, but more could be done. Before we begin to change, we must imagine the possibilities.

MATCHING LIBRARY SERVICES TO CHILDREN'S NEEDS

In a world that is changing so quickly, libraries as institutions could take many forms. Dramatic changes are not likely to be made quickly, but it is worth considering the possibilities before deciding that limitations will keep libraries from changing. Some of the possibilities may be almost impossible to reach, and some may be undesirable, but unless librarians consider many options, they will be unprepared for the future.

It is instructive to look at the revolution in reference services in libraries that has occurred in recent years. When documents were first stored in digital form, they were treated much like print documents. Rigid subject tags were attached, and librarians learned a new vocabulary for online searching. End users were not expected to master the art of finding materials in online formats any more than the average user could find material in print sources. When Google came along, librarians were unprepared for the dramatic impact it would have. In fact, it has changed the face of academic libraries and is modifying many public libraries too.

Google's search engine, developed by private enterprise rather than public institutions, puts every searcher, from elementary school children to reference librarians, in charge of his or her own searches. Information that used to be locked in libraries suddenly became available in classrooms and homes. The results have not all been beneficial. Much misinformation is available on the internet, but the vast majority of the general public and even students are quite content to "Google it" when they have a question rather than ask for help from an expert librarian. As a result, many academic libraries have become "information commons," heavy on computers and less dedicated to print. Librarians still have a very active role to play in choosing and monitoring databases and instructing users in effective searching, but their contribution is often unrecognized. The average person often feels completely capable of finding information individually.

Wikipedia, to a lesser extent, has also revolutionized library services, and its impact came as a surprise to most librarians. After years of evaluating reference tools, examining the credentials of the compilers, and learning the idiosyncrasies of each tool, librarians found themselves usurped by an encyclopedia with thousands of unmonitored contributors. The pattern has changed somewhat as Wikipedia's founders have discovered some of the weaknesses expected by librarians, but Wikipedia's growth continues. Like Google, this innovation came from outside the library world, but it has affected library service far more than many library-initiated projects.

Librarians should learn the lessons of this pattern of innovation coming from outside. Although it is true that government support was needed to make the internet possible, most of its growth has come from commercial sources. The driving force of Google may be to "do no evil," but that is very different from the mission of public libraries to actively do good for the community. The results are mixed. Commercialization of the internet can lead to distortions of information, and this is especially dangerous for children, many of whom are not sophisticated enough to recognize it. Nonetheless, it must give us pause to realize that during the last 15 years, commercial sources have made information more easily available to the average person than public libraries have done during their 100-year history.

In the spirit of considering all possibilities, including some that may seem more like fantasies than possibilities, here is a lost of some possible scenarios for children's services of the future:

1. Traditional library plus enhancement of access to a variety of formats, but with strong emphasis on books and reading
2. Hybrid library with standard buildings but increased emphasis on web access for materials and services
3. Library with physical presence but different presentation—perhaps small units in storefronts, kiosks, coffee shops, shopping malls, schools, or community centers
4. Library differentiated by services but not by age levels—free-flowing between adult and child services
5. Library for children as clubhouse or refuge for children and their caregivers, with access to a variety of formats
6. Entirely digital or online library with access through home or school computers or mobile devices
7. Library building without books—resources available in digital formats but presented in a facility designed for them and with "librarians" acting as information guides
8. Library as a private enterprise supported by membership fees or advertising

Thoughtful librarians can no doubt come up with other possibilities, and the actual future is likely to be different from any prediction. In succeeding chapters, this book looks at how some changes in children's media are affecting today's libraries and how they might impact the future. The possibilities are great, and they increase as innovations in technology, science, and the arts spread quickly through society. The future is exciting, and it can be a bright one for librarians and the children they serve.

SECTION I

CHANGES IN CHILDREN'S LIVES

2

---·◦‣◦·---

HOW HAVE SERVICES TO THE YOUNGEST CHANGED?

Children are born into a world filled with stimulation, what William James famously called "blooming, buzzing confusion." Gradually, they construct for themselves an understanding of the world outside of themselves. The voice and touch of their parents or caregivers are their first introduction to other humans, but soon they learn to interact with other adults and children. Sources of information about the world are limited for young children, but there are many more of them now than there were for earlier generations of children.

WHERE LIBRARIES ARE NOW

Let's look at some of the conventional ways libraries offer services to preschool children today and consider how they might need to change in the new technology environment. Children under the age of six are still called preschoolers because they usually have not entered the public school system. Many of them, however, are enrolled in preschool programs—nursery schools or daycare centers—so often they have more group experiences than children of earlier generations. Nonetheless, for convenience, we will continue to call this group the preschoolers.

The changes that take place in the first three years of life are greater than in any other similar period of life. A newborn baby bears little resemblance to the three-year-old child he or she will become.

To serve children during these years of change, librarians have to understand something about how children grow and develop. Although physical development is very important, librarians are mostly concerned with intellectual and emotional growth. The urge to know and understand the world around them underlies many activities of toddlers. Children are born with what seems to be an innate desire to make sense of their environment. The role of adults is to help children to make this sense. We have to start early. The years up to age three are very important years of growth. The role of language is crucial in the growth of young children, and many library services are devoted to encouraging language development.

Infant	Three-year-old	Five-year-old
Unable to feed self	Feeds self with occasional help	Eats independently; chooses food
Unable to speak	Talks in short sentences	Talks fluently
Unable to recognize people	Understands much of the language heard	Understands many adult conversations and participates
Unable to walk or even move without help	Walks easily	Walks, runs, rides small bicycles

Figure 2.1 Changes in the first five years.

Programs for Babies and Toddlers

Storyhours for babies, often called lapsit programs, are one of the success stories of children's services. As more and more parents learn about the value of reading and word play for infants, libraries are offering more programs for babies. These not only are valuable for the children, but also accustom the family to the idea of using library programs as part of their child-rearing practices. Parents who have a few weeks or months of parental leave from work can get some experience of children's library programs while they are spending more time at home. Often, these parents encourage babysitters and daycare centers to continue using library programs as the children grow older. Many baby programs are designed for children from birth to 18 months of age. A few library systems limit the age to under 12 months and offer separate programs for 12- to 18-month-old children.

Programs for Infants

Infants cannot talk or understand spoken language, but that doesn't mean they are not affected by it. Listening to the sounds of the language spoken around them teaches them to distinguish between different sounds. When their babbling gets a response, they gradually learn that language can affect what happens. They can bring a smile to a parent's face or even get food by making noises. This may not seem like an intellectual breakthrough, but what it does is change the perception of the world from a random assortment of noises and sights into something that can be affected by an individual's action. Understanding that they can influence other people by consciously making noises offers a huge incentive for learning language. That is the reason children raised in solitude, or in greatly restricted conditions where they don't get feedback from adults, lose much of their mental ability during the first few years of life. Children in normal household settings learn they can make a difference and affect their environment—the beginning of power.

One of the most crucial steps in learning language occurs when a child is about 18 months of age—the recognition that every object has a name. Researcher Maryanne Wolf writes, "The special quality of this insight is based on the brain's ability to connect two or more systems to make something new" (2008, p. 24). Simple naming activities help a child develop this insight and are a first step in learning to read.

Once they grasp the relationship between words and entities in the world, children start learning words at an amazing rate. Scientists believe that the average child between the ages of two and five learns an average of two to four words each day. This foundation of language learning is the basis of a decades-long intellectual growth. Many libraries provide programs for children from birth onward. Following is the description of the baby programs given at Multnomah County Public Libraries (2010):

> Babies from birth to 12 months (with a favorite adult) enjoy songs, action rhymes, and playtime and share a book together in each lively Book Babies session. Book Babies gives your baby the opportunity to hear lots of language while you get to know other young families.

Lapsit programs rely on auditory, visual, and sensory approaches. Children hear the sounds of language and music, see adults doing finger plays and gesturing to express emotion, and feel the sensory pleasure of sitting in a familiar, sheltering lap and the adventure of having their hands clapped together or placed over their eyes or mouth. This is an exciting change from the enforced immobility of lying in a crib or even sitting in a stroller while being pushed around streets or a shopping mall.

The value of structured lapsit programs for babies over the stimulation of a stroller ride through a shopping mall is that the program is geared toward the level of the child. Instead of the overstimulation of bright lights, chattering crowds, and often loud music, there is quiet talk directed at the individual child. These programs are short, usually between 20 and 30 minutes, because babies have short attention spans. They lose interest and cry or fall asleep if the program lasts too long. If a baby fusses or cries during the program, the caregiver is encouraged to speak softly to the child and try to soothe her. If the crying becomes too obtrusive, a caregiver may remove the child from the group and walk around the room or leave. As babies become accustomed to the programs, this doesn't happen very often.

See Figure 2.2 for an example of what a storyhour program for the youngest group might look like.

Toddler Programs

As children become toddlers (18 to 36 months), they are more often cared for in groups. Many toddlers have two working parents and spend at least several hours or days each week being cared for in a group. Because most librarians believe it is no longer necessary to have one caregiver per child, the nature of the library program changes. Toddlers can walk and move around on their own, but their actions are not easily controlled by verbal directions. Often, a toddler who is doing something unacceptable, such as pulling books down from a shelf, has to be physically removed from the temptation. Just saying "no" is not enough. Somewhere between the ages of two and three, toddlers learn to respond to verbal directions, and this too is an important step forward in language development.

Some libraries require a caregiver to accompany each child, but this often means children in any type of group care are unable to participate. In some communities, this may eliminate most of the audience for a program. If a toddler program requires one adult present for each child, it should probably be scheduled for early

BABY TIME PROGRAM
GRASSHOPPER VALLEY PUBLIC LIBRARY

Audience: Limited to 15 caregivers each with a baby (plus an older sibling if necessary)

Preparation:

- Place 15 carpet samples or baby blankets on floor for sitting or use chairs in a circle.
- Gather books ahead of time and place them on speaker's table or use a pocket apron.
- Prepare attractive list of books and activities used to distribute to caregivers. (Also make this available on the website.)
- Gather together toys for babies to handle after program.

Introduction: Librarian welcomes participants and provides a sheet with words for the songs and title and location information for caregivers.

Welcome Song: Librarian sings,

"Good morning to you!
Good morning to you
Good morning, dear [child's name]
Good morning to you"

First story: *Brown Bear, Brown Bear What Do You See* by Bill Martin

Action Rhyme: "Open, Shut Them"

Open, shut them, open, shut them (open and close hands)
Give a little clap, clap, clap! (clap hands)
Open, shut them, open, shut them,
Lay them in your lap! (lay hands in lap)

Second story: *Jamberry* by Bruce Deegen

Action Rhyme: "If You're Happy and You Know It"

If you're happy and you know it, clap your hands (clap hands)
If you're happy and you know it, clap your hands!
If you're happy and you know it, and you really want to show it,
If you're happy and you know it, clap your hands!

Playtime: Soft toys are distributed for babies to play with for 5 or 10 minutes.

End: Say goodbye and encourage people to come again. Remind caregivers that the titles and words of songs are available on the children's department homepage.

Figure 2.2   Sample baby-time program.

evening or on weekends. Many libraries have found that a ratio of one adult for every two or three toddlers is manageable for short programs.

Programs for toddlers can be longer than those for babies; a typical program might last 30 minutes. When planning a program for toddlers, librarians want to remember the developmental changes in the children:

- Toddlers can walk and move on their own, so the programs should allow children to stretch their muscles—to stand up, wriggle, and jump or walk.
- Motor activities should be accompanied by rhymes or songs so the children have a chance to use their language skills.
- Books that take advantage of the toddlers' fast-growing language abilities should be chosen. Following are some desirable qualities:

  1. Familiar subject: The everyday world is fascinating to young children. They may be confused by fantasy or exotic settings.
  2. Large, clear, bright-colored pictures.
  3. Simple plots: Some books are only pictures with labels on them. These give toddlers a chance to exercise their new skill in labeling.
  4. Clear, simple words: There should be just a few words on each page. Toddlers like books when words are fun to say, and phrases are repeated.

Programs for Preschoolers

By the time children are three years old, most of them can communicate easily with adults about everyday events and can understand much of what is going on around them. They are moving beyond the labeling of objects and seeing pictures individually. They are learning to see patterns and follow the sequence of activities and understand why one thing follows another. This is a crucial step forward in their intellectual development. Jane Healy writes,

> After years of studying young children's learning, I am increasingly convinced that *patterns* are the key to intelligence. Patterning information really means organizing and associating new information with previously developed mental hooks. (2004, p. 61)

Library services to preschoolers should encourage them to find patterns, to see connections between things. That is the reason for choosing a theme for a preschool storyhour. Children are delighted to recognize connections. You might hear one say, "The monkeys in that story are just like the silly monkeys in the song we sang."

The librarian can take advantage of this by helping children see connections: After reading *Miss Spider's Tea Party* by David Kirk, the librarian might say, "We just read a story about a friendly spider. Now here's a little rhyme about a different spider called 'Incy Wincy Spider.'" This kind of conversation ties the experiences together and gives children a sense of the connections between different media experiences.

GRASSHOPPER VALLEY PUBLIC LIBRARY

Theme: Funny Birds

Opening Song:

Oh, the duck says "Quack,"
and the cow says "Moo."
The old red rooster says
"Cock-a-doodle-doo."
The sheep says "Baa,"
and the cat says "Meow,"
but I say "Good morning"
when I see you!

Adapted from http://www.canteach.ca/elementary/songspoems68.html

First story: *Duck on a Bike* by David Shannon

Action Rhyme:

Ten little ducklings,
Dash, dash, dash!
Jumped in the duck pond,
Splash, splash, splash!
When the mother called them,
"Quack, quack, quack!"
Ten little ducklings
Swam right back.

Retrieved from http://www.canteach.ca/elementary/songspoems58.html

Second story: *Don't Let the Pigeon Drive the Bus* by Mo Willems

Action Rhyme:

　"The Wheels on the Bus"

Third story: *Truck Duck* by Michael Rex

Craft Activity:

Give out the following supplies:

- large sheets of paper
- crayon boxes
- smaller sheets of colored paper
- safe scissors
- discarded magazines for cutting up
- paste sticks

Ask the children to make pictures of birds, insects, or animals riding on bikes, cars, or other vehicles. When they are finished, they take the pictures home.

Figure 2.3　Sample preschool program.

As children's attention span grows, the programs can be longer, especially if the stories are broken up with brief activities. Often, the program ends with a craft. Children love to have something to take home for their family, and the craft object serves as a reminder of the library and the programs there. It can help make the library a presence in the home.

ELECTRONIC ENHANCEMENTS FOR PROGRAMMING

The sample programs in Figures 2.2 and 2.3 are typical of programs being given in many libraries, but it is noticeable that the materials and activities are similar to ones that could have been done 10 or even 20 years ago. Electronic services have revolutionized many aspects of library service, but they have had little impact on services for young children in most libraries. Yet we know that children's lives are influenced by the influx of electronic media in their homes. Let's look at some of the ways media have changed for young children.

The changing media environment of young children has been a controversial subject for many people. Librarians have traditionally been strong advocates of children's reading. Children's libraries were founded with the purpose of encouraging children to read. As Virginia Walter notes, librarians were firm believers in the "conviction that books and reading are essential to the human spirit" (2001, p. 1). In their zeal to promote reading, some libraries have been hostile to other media forms as they have been introduced. When movies became available early in the 20th century and when radio then entered people's homes during the 1920s, both were feared as dangerous rivals to reading. The introduction of television during the 1950s led to even greater anxiety.

None of the concerns of critics have stopped ongoing changes in the media world. Because television is a part of almost every American household, children have their first experience with it at a very young age. A Kaiser Family Foundation study of children up to age six reports, "Nearly all children (99%) live in a home with a TV set, half (50%) have three or more TVs, and one-third (36%) have a TV in their bedroom" (Rideout 2003, p. 4). Some research has been done on the

In the Home	In the Library
Ubiquitous music (MP3 player, radio, computer)	No noise except quiet voices
Visual images from TV playing constantly	No moving images
Computer available for quick lookups or a video game	Computers have to be reserved in advance
Cell phone for texting or calling friends	Use of cell phones often not allowed
Very few books available in most homes	Wide range of books available

Figure 2.4   Media differences between home and library.

amount of exposure to electronic media experienced by preschool children. One of the few studies available that includes preschoolers suggests the exposure may be greater than generally assumed. Researchers have found that one-fifth of newborns to two-year-olds and more than one-third of three-year-olds to six-year-olds have a television set in their bedroom. Parents often explain that the purpose of this set for such a young child is to soothe and distract the child (Vandewater et al. 2007, p. 1). During the early 2000s, videos for infants became a popular purchase for middle-class families. Some companies promised that watching specially designed videos could stimulate an infant's brain and lead to an increased intelligence. After several years of good sales, Disney began offering rebates to families who had purchased the videos, admitting there was no proof that these videos increased a child's intelligence. This had a dampening effect on sales of the product but probably did not decrease the amount of television watched in the home. Whether or not videos can stimulate intelligence, there is no question that they interest children and can keep them quiet.

The prevalence of television viewing by children younger than two goes against the advice of the American Academy of Pediatrics (1999, p. 342), which recommends that children have no exposure to television until they reach the age of three. These guidelines were issued in 1999 at a time when many homes did not have as many television sets as they do now. Babies who spend their time in the living room or kitchen with parents are almost inevitably exposed to television. Parents themselves often explain their provision of television for very young children by saying that it calms the toddlers or provides something interesting to watch. The use of the television as a babysitter has been criticized in many media channels, but it is still common practice in many homes. The question of why parents differ from the experts on this facet of their children's lives would be a valuable one to study.

Bridging the Gap between Home Media and Library Media

Librarians could easily feel quite smug about providing the kinds of programs that many parents are not offering their children at home. Excluding electronic media follows guidelines set by many child development experts. So are conventional library programs perfectly attuned to families today? Perhaps we ought to consider whether, by shutting out this form of media and extolling the virtues of books, we may be creating an unfortunate division between the library and the home—even perhaps between the library and the rest of the child's world. It is important not to set up the library as the enemy of other media because children are going to have to live in a multimedia world.

Varying the Mix in Collections

What can libraries do to integrate library resources with the resources that children and their families use outside the library? Both collections and services can reflect the realities of how modern families live.

- Include electronic as well as print versions of picture books in the collection through offering DVDs, streaming video on the library website, and apps for mobile devices. (Picture book apps—short for applications—are the fastest-growing format for picture books and are being produced by many mainstream publishers.)

- Provide a wide range of audiobooks.
- On booklists, include websites that offer children's books online and apps that can be downloaded for mobile formats.
- Have booklists of picture books available in ebook format for parents to download.
- Encourage parents to interact with their children on computers rather than making computer use a solitary experience.

Adding to the Mix in Programming

Instead of following traditional storyhour choices, librarians can integrate multimedia into some of the programs offered to preschool children. This builds on what most children are accustomed to having available at home.

This program doesn't differ greatly from the programs outlined previously, but there are subtle shifts that bridge the gap between a book-rich library and a media-rich home. Many libraries use videos in programming for children and have done so for years. Fewer libraries carry through on this and add videos, ebooks, and audiobooks to the reading lists distributed to parents. Much of the media still presents the library as a book-centered institution presided over by serious librarians who read much more than most people do. What librarian has not been disconcerted occasionally when, upon telling a new acquaintance that he or she is a librarian, discovers that the immediate reaction is an apologetic account of what a good thing reading is—if only there were time to do it? Parents take their children to libraries to encourage their reading, but at the same time, in many households, reading remains an alien activity. Reading is work—watching television is fun. Libraries should try to demonstrate that all forms of media are respected, and all formats for reading and interacting with books are encouraged by libraries.

Preschool children are usually enthusiastic about books and reading. The overwhelming majority of them enjoy going to the library. They look forward to learning to read. Smart librarians take advantage of this enthusiasm to make the library and its services an integral part of family life. This includes showing respect for the favorite media of children and parents and integrating varied formats into library services.

Using Interactive Media to Facilitate Services

The child is only half of the picture in services to preschoolers; children are served best when their parents and caregivers are included in the plan for library services. In today's world, the parents and caregivers of young children may be interested in helping them gain access to print media, but most of them are dependent on other formats for everyday information. They will appreciate the library's efforts to communicate with them by the most comfortable format available. This does not mean giving up the channels that have worked for years, but rather being ready to examine new possibilities. How can libraries best use media to communicate?

Traditional Outlets for Information about Library Services

1. Know the media that parents of young children use to find out about community activities. Balance the effectiveness of each medium with its cost.

GRASSHOPPER VALLEY PUBLIC LIBRARY
MULTIMEDIA PROGRAM FOR PRESCHOOLERS
THEME: SPIDERS

Opening Song: "Good Morning to You"

Story: *Anansi the Spider* by Gerald McDermott

Rhyme: "We're Going on a Spider Hunt" (based on "We're Going on a Lion Hunt")

                  I'm going on a spider hunt.
                  I'm going on a spider hunt *(slap thighs)*.
                  I see a swamp *(shade eyes with hand)*.
                  Can't go under it.
                  Can't go over it.
                  Must go through it.

Slush, slush, slush *(follow the leader around in a small circle pretending to wade through water)*.

(The librarian can make up verses as they go along, seeing a bridge, a stream, or whatever seems appropriate)

DVD screening: *Diary of a Spider* (Weston Woods 2008)

Action Rhyme: "Incy Bincy Spider"

Craft: Hand out large sheets of paper, string, glue sticks, and crayons. Children can make spider webs to paste to the paper and then draw background and spiders with the crayons. If possible, have small black pompoms to paste on paper as bodies for the spider.

Handouts for Parents and Caregivers: Include list of books and DVDs about spiders. Mention that Tumblebooks and other ebooks in the library include tales about spiders and other creatures.

Figure 2.5 Sample multimedia program for preschoolers.

Try to find the least expensive way to get out your message, perhaps by sharing the resources of other groups. Many parent–teacher associations have e-newsletters that accept program notices from other organizations. Some churches and civic organizations are also willing to post notices about library services.

2. Don't neglect the traditional print notices about programs, such as through flyers in the library branches and bookmobiles. Distribute flyers to schools and daycare centers. Print notices in community newspapers

3. Keep the children's page of the library website current by posting all notices about children's services and programs promptly. It is vital to keep these notices current and remove activities as they are completed.

Those who have come of age with cell phones and social media are skilled at arranging their social life on a "just in time" basis, the way many businesses handle their supplies. The traditional rules about replying to invitations and making firm time commitments no longer apply for many of them. This means that librarians cannot expect a high rate of response if they ask parents to sign up for activities in advance. Most libraries have given up asking for registration for storyhours and other programs and allow last-minute decisions about attending. The librarian has to know the community and experiment to decide which approach works best locally.

Using Interactive Outlets for Information

1. Use Facebook and other social media. Library Facebook pages are a relatively new development in library services, and they can be developed as an important part of library publicity plans because many people visit the site at least once a day. Posting notices of an event or an addition to the collection takes very little staff time and can be effective. Sending evites to a self-selected group of fans is also easy, although response rates tend to be low. Videos and podcasts of programs can be posted, as can the lyrics to songs or titles of books.
2. Text messages about programs can be sent to cell phones and mobile devices. An automatic cell phone reminder can go out on the morning of the program to people who have signed up for it. (Note: be sure to allow individuals to opt out of any automatic messages planned.)
3. More and more libraries are allowing patrons (or their parents) to get library news on Twitter. Sending a tweet about an upcoming event is a good reminder for people who follow Twitter accounts, and many young parents do.

Encouraging Ongoing Adult Engagement in Children's Programming

Depending on how consistent a group forms for the preschool programming, it may be worthwhile to offer more permanent groups for parents. These can take several forms:

1. *Face-to-face social group in the library.* In some communities, a preschool parents' group can meet weekly or monthly. The meeting can be held during the storytime if children can be left on their own, or it can be held at another time when parents have babysitting available, or when one member of the group takes responsibility for entertaining the children while other parents meet. Under this arrangement parents usually rotate the responsibility.
2. *Online discussion groups.* If a leader can be found among the parents, the librarians can encourage parents to form an online group. Companies such as Google and Yahoo! offer free group sites that can be quickly formed and require very little monitoring.
3. *Special page on library webpage.* On the children's department webpage, the librarian can set up a section for parents. This would include links to useful websites for parents. It could also host a blog open to parents for comments and questions related to library programs, materials, and parenting.

A group such as Friends of the Library could be responsible for the blog if there is a willing volunteer. Examples of informative children's webpages include the following:

- Chicago (Illinois) Public Library has lists of resources for parents, including homeschooling and autism resources. http://www.chipublib.org/forkids/index.php/.
- Santa Monica (California) Public Library has a page of resources for parents and one for teachers. http://www.smplkids.org/.
- Brooklyn (New York) Public Library separates its youth pages into three sections—teen, children, and under-fives. The under-five page suggests reading and includes parenting tips and collections of rhymes and finger plays that parents can use with children. http://www.brooklynpublicli brary.org/kids_teens.jsp/.

4. *Programming for parents.* In addition to programs for children and families, libraries have often been successful with programs aimed at parents. Many other community groups serve the parents of young children and may be willing to cosponsor these programs. Many groups have ideas for programs but find it difficult to locate an inexpensive place in which to hold them. Libraries usually have meeting rooms where community groups can be accommodated, so it is a natural partnership. Sources of speakers for these programs include social agencies, health care providers, universities, and government agencies. Topics might include the following:

- Issues in health care such as vaccinations or infectious disease
- Nutrition, food safety, menus
- Behavior problems and how to deal with them
- Effect of television or other media on children
- Obesity
- Innovations in education

5. *Blogs for children and parents.* Many public libraries have started blogs, and some have blogs aimed at young children and their parents. This is a good, participatory means of encouraging parents to remain involved with the library. Lists of new books can be posted on a blog as they come into the collection; programs can be announced; publicity can be given to community events. Blogs are meant to be interactive, and parental participation should be encouraged. Far more people read blogs than add comments to them, but even a small group of active participants can make for a lively blog. Some good examples include the following:

- Booth and Dimock Memorial Library, http://dreyfusdragon.blogspot.com/
- Des Plaines Public Library, http://kidding-around.blogspot.com/
- Fauquier County Public Library, http://kiddosphere.blogspot.com/

There is almost no end to the variety of methods libraries have used to reach out to parents. It is important for libraries to be aware of possibilities.

POINTS ABOUT PRESCHOOLERS

Young children come to the library with no preconceived ideas about what it will be like. Often, their parents have very little idea of what libraries are like either, but both young children and young parents are eager to learn. The preschool years are probably the best opportunity for a librarian to establish a long-lasting relationship between the library and the family. The traditional collections and programs of a library prepare a child for reading and enjoying books. Newer technology can help librarians link to parents and caregivers and provide useful connections that make the library part of their busy lives and not a remote old-fashioned institution. Good services for preschoolers build a solid foundation for children and libraries.

3

WHAT HAS CHANGED FOR CHILDREN FROM FIVE TO NINE?

The beginning of formal education is one of the most important milestones in childhood. When children enter school, they start on the important intellectual task of learning to read. Reading changes the brain and enables people to learn in different ways; it also changes the ways children interact with the world, giving them a new power to manipulate machines and understand communication. Another dramatic change in children's lives at this time is the gradual disappearance of parents. Peers become more important figures, and children strive to be accepted in the social group. Unfortunately, it is often at this time that libraries reduce their services to children. Many children start thinking of the library as a place to do homework and study instead of a place to enjoy new experiences.

STARTING SCHOOL AND THE CHANGES THAT BRINGS

When children enter "real" school, which is usually the primary grades of elementary school, they are expected to learn many new skills and acquire new knowledge, but the most important intellectual achievement of primary school is learning to read. Even though preliminary reading skills, such as letter recognition, may be taught in preschool, the primary grades of elementary school provide many children's first encounter with formal reading instruction. Learning to read will be the key to their future education, and as Maryann Wolf writes, "how a child first learns to read is a tale of either magic and fairies or missed chances and unnecessary loss" (2007, p. 82).

Instead of listening to storyhours in library programs, school children are expected to encounter books on their own and extract information and entertainment for themselves. Reading requires the brain to establish different pathways to understanding. We are only beginning to understand why literacy makes such a difference to individuals and societies as scientists learn more about how the human brain works.

The Difference Reading Makes

Children learn to understand and speak language by living in a society that uses language. Every four-year-old throughout the world, except for those with serious mental or physical impairment, will learn the spoken language used in the community. Very few children learn to read spontaneously, perhaps 1 or 2 percent of the population (Margrain 2006, p. 1). Most children must be taught to read, and this is often a laborious process. For centuries, it was assumed that only a small, select group of people would learn to read. No one considered reading a mass skill until the 19th century, when the development of an industrial society made a literate population desirable. Now we expect every child to learn to read fluently, and those who do not acquire reading easily are often shunted off the track to higher education and better jobs. Although reading is usually considered a personal achievement and the hallmark of a cultured person, it has also become an economic necessity.

When a child learns to read, he or she gains the power to interact with media directly instead of relying on an adult to read and interpret. Reading is one of the first steps toward giving a child control of a world outside the home. Many eminent people have talked about what learning to read means to children.

Alberto Manguel writes, "The child learning to read is admitted into the communal memory by way of books, and thereby becomes acquainted with a common past which he or she renews, to a greater or lesser degree, in every reading" (1996, p. 71). And Rumor Godden noted that "when you learn to read you will be born again . . . and you will never be quite so alone again" (Wolf 2007, p. 109). Fiction echoes the same theme, as shown in the perennial favorite *A Tree Grows in Brooklyn*: "From that time on, the world was hers for the reading. She would never be lonely again, never miss the lack of intimate friends. Books became her friends and there was one for every mood" (Smith 1943, p. 140).

Learning to Read

Going to school and learning to read changes a child's world in many subtle ways, but not all children find the learning easy or straightforward. Ordinarily, teachers expect children to learn to read fluently during the first three years of elementary school. To be prepared for reading, a child should have already mastered several important skills:

- Knowing how to speak the language
- Knowing that print represents language
- Knowing that to read in English, the eye moves from left to right across the page
- Knowing that letters represent sounds

Children who have been read to during their preschool years and who have engaged in conversations with adults have learned these things. Library storyhours hone these skills and help children associate reading and books with fun. Children who have not had these experiences are likely to have a more difficult time catching up and being ready for reading when it becomes necessary.

Reading skills are increasingly being taught in preschool and kindergarten, although not all experts agree that early reading is an advantage to a child's education. The California Curriculum standards' (http://www.cde.ca.gov/ci/) description of skills a child should develop in kindergarten includes the following:

- Concepts about print
- Phonemic awareness
- Decoding and word recognition
- Vocabulary and concept development

Although libraries do not have a direct role to play in teaching a child to read, they can help lay the framework for these essential skills. Most libraries devote much of their programming time and effort to helping preschool children develop some of the necessary pre-reading skills, but often they step back at the crucial time when children are moving on to independent reading. Programming for school-age children is not offered in as many libraries as programming for preschoolers. Some communities, but not all, have strong school libraries to fill the gap, but education budgets in recent years have led to cutbacks in school library programs in many districts.

Practical Value of Reading

Reading is a practical and important skill in today's society. Modern education depends on fluent literacy, and education is the gateway to economic independence. But reading is seen as much more than that in modern society, especially in the humanistic circles in which most librarians move. Reading is often viewed as an inherently virtuous activity by educators and librarians, and reading is often equated with reading books. Most studies of leisure activities, however, show that the majority of Americans do not read many books and have no desire to do so. One 2008 study documented an unexpected rise in the percentage of people who read literature, but the figure is still only 50.2 percent ("Reading on Rise" 2008, p. 4). Perhaps librarians should shift their attention away from trying to make children become avid readers of books and concentrate instead on encouraging reading skills that could be deployed in a number of different media. It's important for librarians to know not only about children's books and reading but also about the whole ever-changing media world of children today.

CHANGING MEDIA WORLD OF SCHOOL-AGE CHILDREN

Traditional Media

- *Stories in books*—the most highly respected media for children. Books are not available in all children's homes, but they are freely available in schools and libraries, and their use is strongly encouraged by adults
- *Television*—the most pervasive medium in most homes. About 98 percent of American homes have television; many have multiple sets. Although television is

sometimes deplored by educators and media critics, most parents accept it as an important part of family life. Many children have TV sets in their bedrooms and have freedom to choose which shows they will watch. Although parents have the ability to monitor their children's television use, many do not.

- *CDs*—fading fast as the method for distributing recorded music. Some homes and schools still have CDs, but most children turn to MP3 players.

New Forms of Media

- *Computers*—Access to computers is almost universal for American children. In 2009, 93 percent of 8-to 18-year-olds lived in a home that had a computer, and 84 percent had internet access at home. Almost a third of children over 8 years of age own their own laptop. As families increase the number of computers in the home, children are often given the older machines, so access is likely to increase with time. The minority of children who do not have computers at home have access to them in schools and libraries (Rideout, Foehr, and Roberts 2010).

- *Reading ebooks*—Libraries and schools encourage the use of some ebooks, especially online reference books. For younger children, the Digital Children's Library offers short story books from many cultures. As they grow older, many children find their own books online, especially science fiction books and comic books. Kindles have been adopted in some school districts as an alternative to textbooks. Although ebooks account for only a small percentage of book reading in 2010, their use is likely to become more widespread.

- *MP3 players*—The CD collections in libraries are often unused as more and more people, including young children, prefer to download music from the internet. With the availability of inexpensive MP3 players, music has become a ubiquitous form of media for children. Choosing and editing music on their mobile devices is a way for young people to manage their image and impress their friends. Choosing their own music is one of the earliest ways children have of declaring their independence from family choices.

- *Playaways*—This is a format used in libraries and schools, but almost never in homes. These audio versions of books that come complete with a listening device are economical if they are used by many people, but not for individual use. Some schools are encouraging children to listen to these books while they are walking on a track or around the gym so that some exercise can be combined with reading.

- *Gaming*—Many children learn to play computer games at a young age. Websites designed for young children, including library websites, often link to educational games. When children start school, they often spend time playing non-educational video games either on websites or on designated video game players. More than 80 percent of families with children ages 8 to 18 have video game players in the home, and more than 50 percent of these children have them in their own room.

- *Social networking*—School-age children often start using social networks. There are several, such as Club Penguin and Webkinz, designed for young children. The largest networks such as Facebook and MySpace are designed for teenagers and adults, but some children may join them earlier than the suggested guidelines.

What Does the Proliferation of Media Mean to Libraries?

Although children live in a media-saturated world, libraries do not always integrate these media into their services. The traditional media of books, CDs, videos, and DVDs are available as part of most children's collections. Playaways are increasingly being offered. Computers are available in most children's departments, and catalogs are, of course, computer-based. Databases and reference tools are available online, and their use is encouraged, but the wealth of materials on the internet is not often considered part of library resources.

Consider the difference between a child's life outside the library and the one found inside. If you look back at Figure 2.4, "Media Differences between Home and Library," in the preceding chapter, you will recall the differences between the library and the outside world of media in which the child lives. School-age children are likely to notice this difference even more than preschoolers. For the majority of children, a large and varied book collection is the only advantage in terms of media availability that the library offers, and although books are very important, the collection leaves out many other media sources of entertainment and information that children are accustomed to. It is small wonder that as children advance in school, they tend to think of public and school libraries solely as educational resources to be used when needed, not as an integral part of their lives.

Another notable fact about children's use of media is that different kinds of media are often used at the same time. Music on MP3 players accompanies most activities, including reading, doing homework, and riding the school bus or walking to school. Television is often turned on as soon as a child walks into his or her room after school and is left on for the rest of the day. Homework, reading, telephone calls, texting, and computer use all take place against the background of a television screen.

Still another feature of children's media use is that many of the new media are interactive. Reading a library book in which scribbling comments is strongly discouraged is essentially a physically passive activity, no matter how much mental activity it may generate. From a child's point of view, reading a book involves taking something in, not reacting to it. In this way it is very much like watching television. Many of the newer media encourage participation and reaction. The plot of a video game is moved along by the player, who has a strong impact on the actions that follow. The choice of songs and their sequence on MP3 playlists reflect the user's preferences. Texting obviously requires a response and functions through interaction. On a computer, the user chooses which links to follow on a webpage and can flip from one to another to follow a narrative or choose particular aspects of a subject to follow. The impact these differences should have on a library's program are discussed further later in this chapter.

THE DISAPPEARING PARENT

Parents are the most important people in a young child's life. They may be one or two of the biological parents or grandparents, adoptive parents, or caregivers who fill the parental role in the day-to-day life of a child. Young children need adults to watch over their early development as they learn language and social skills. As children enter school and learn how to socialize with their peers and with adults outside the family circle, they rely less on parents for their daily life.

Growing Importance of Peer Group

As children take their first steps toward independence from their families, their peers become increasingly important. Socializing successfully with other children is an important step in adjusting to school. Children who get along well with their peers usually do better academically than those who find it difficult to mingle. Peer groups form for various activities, and being accepted by these groups becomes an important goal. Adults may find it difficult to adjust to being of secondary importance in children's lives, but gaining independence from adults is a necessary step for children as they grow up.

Gender Becomes More Important

Another change that occurs during the early grades is the formation of gender-based groups. Girls and boys often separate and move into different activities. Even when teachers and other adults encourage boys and girls to work together on projects, recreational activities tend to become strongly gender-based. Any adult who attempts to organize activities for preteen children has to decide whether to go along with this tendency and set up separate groups for boys and girls or whether to try to ignore the differences and encourage mixed groups. These decisions can have far-reaching effects on the success of library programs.

WHAT LIBRARIES ARE DOING FOR SCHOOL-AGE CHILDREN

Programming is not offered as frequently for school-age children as it is for the preschoolers. Storyhours and programs for very young children are usually the most popular programs in libraries, and they sometimes use all of the energy and resources that children's department staff can muster for programming. Librarians find it easier to present preschool programs because they can often be offered at times when the library would otherwise be quiet and unused. The free time that schoolchildren have coincides with the busiest hours of library use for everyone.

After-School Programs

A variety of after-school programs are offered in libraries. A few libraries work with schools or other community groups to present an active program of activities throughout the week. Many other libraries set aside one or two afternoons per week to invite school-age children for special activities. The most frequently sponsored activities are designed to help children in school and to improve their reading skills.

Homework Help

Many homework help centers promoted by libraries on their website or in the branches are listings of resources that children can use to find information for school projects. The Multnomah County (Oregon) Public Library, for example, lists the library databases as well as recommended websites for children to use (http://www.multcolib.org/homework/). Many other libraries offer similar webpages listing informative materials for children to use in their homework.

Online homework help is also a popular resource in many libraries. Miami Dade County Public Library offers lists of links to informative websites and also an "Ask a Librarian" tab that allows young people to email a question or to chat live with a librarian (http://www.mdpls.org/).

Homework help centers in the library building are also available in some libraries. These centers may be staffed by librarians or volunteers. Some libraries have recruited high school students to work with younger students and help them with homework. The Boston Public Library's Homework Assistance Program is an example of an organized program to facilitate this tutoring. As described on the library's website, students are offered help in a range of subject areas.

HOMEWORK ASSISTANCE PROGRAM (HAP)

- Free drop-in tutoring
- Available in all subject areas to students in grades K–8
- Provided by high-achieving high school student mentors from Boston's public and private school

From http://www.bpl.org/homework/.

In a program funded by the Chicago Public Library Foundation, the library offers a program called "Teachers in the Library" in which teachers are paid to be available to children who drop into the library after school for help with their homework. Any elementary school child can go to the library after school and find help with homework and tutoring in a variety of subjects (http://www.chipublib.org/eventsprog/programs/teach_inlibrary.php). Funding for a program like this would be difficult for most libraries to find without the help of an outside foundation or agency.

Other After-School Programming

Although homework help services are the most frequently offered programs for school-age children, a few public libraries offer one or more recreational programs. Following are some typical programs:

- Game afternoons—board games or computer games
- Craft sessions
- Reading groups

Reading groups are a particularly popular format, perhaps because they have an educational purpose as well as offer recreation. Groups for the five-to-nine age group are often divided by gender because boys and girls often prefer different books. Some groups include parents in mother–daughter or father–daughter configurations. Just as with adult reading groups, more females than males participate, although there are some successful "Guys Read" groups. The leader of such a group may be an adult volunteer or a librarian, or for the eight-and-older age group, children may be in charge. Some groups are organized for a limited period—for example, a summer reading group—whereas others are continuous. Online reading groups organized by outside commercial organizations are hosted in some libraries for school-age children.

Summer Reading Programs

The most widespread recreational library program for school-age children is the summer reading program. These programs are in great demand among parents and teachers because there is a large body of research showing the benefits of summer reading. Almost all children lose some of their educational skills during the long summer school break, but children who continue to read during the summer months do not lose nearly as much as those who do not. In fact, much of the education gap between different economic groups in America can be explained by the fact that many middle-class children continue to learn during the summer, whereas many children from a poverty background, many of them from ethnic minority groups, do not so often learn information relevant to school when they are not in school. As Malcolm Gladwell writes, "Virtually all of the advantage that wealthy students have over poor students is the result of differences in ways privileged kids learn while they are not in school" (2008, p. 258).

Research has shown that "on average, middle-income students experience slight gains in reading performance over the summer months. Low-income students experience an average summer learning loss in reading achievement of over two months" (Cooper, Nye, Charlton, Lindsay, and Greathouse 1996, p. 227). Public libraries have been effective in closing this gap, as documented in the recent study *Public Library Summer Reading Programs Close the Reading Gap* (Roman, Carran, and Fiore 2010).

Continuing to learn over the summer months is not the only reason for having summer reading programs, of course. Summer reading programs offer stimulating fun for children during the long summer break when time can often drag. They offer a free activity for many children whose only other alternative entertainment might be watching television programs. The summer reading program also gives publicity to the library and encourages children and families to continue using the public library. They are a great public relations tool for libraries.

Large library districts, counties, and states often sponsor unified summer reading programs to provide materials for local and branch libraries to use in the summer reading program. The structure of summer reading programs varies, but the common components have been described this way: "The summer reading program is basically a drop-in program where children get a reading log or journal to keep track of books, pages, or time spent reading to show the library to get prizes and other incentives" (Peck 2006, p. 90).

Features of a Summer Reading Program

- Selecting theme
- Publicizing events

- Signing up participants
- Recording progress
- Celebrating completion

Selecting a theme that will appeal to the target age group is the first major task of a summer reading program. Many themes are based on linking books to adventure and exploration. General ideas such as exploring space or discovering new worlds can be tied in with current events or recent popular books. Harry Potter and Percy Jackson are two of the characters who have been used as the basis for several summer reading programs.

Individual libraries and small library systems usually work with larger regional or national groups to develop themes and materials for summer reading programs. Children and parents used to the glossy standards of commercial advertising may not be impressed by local handmade publicity efforts, so using professionals is seen as a more effective choice. Some library groups such as the Collaborative Summer Library Program plan far ahead to involve well-known illustrators and writers to work on their materials. Their themes for summer 2010—"Make a splash at your library: READ" and "Make waves at your library: READ"—were announced in *School Library Journal* in November 2008, two years before the programs were to start.

Many companies market themes and materials for use in library programs. This is a useful way for small libraries to obtain professionally produced publicity materials without using a great deal of staff time. Friends of the Library groups or businesses in the community can be encouraged to support the cost of these efforts.

Publicizing the program to local families is a vital part of organizing a summer reading program. Traditional in-house publicity through flyers and notices to local schools usually attracts the same group of families who participate in other library activities. Although it is gratifying that children who are already library users enjoy signing up for special summer programs, most libraries would like to encourage nonusers to participate too. Getting the word out beyond the libraries usually involves efforts such as the following:

- Notices on the library website
- News releases to local newspapers and radio stations
- Ads in local newspapers
- Flyers to all schools including private and religious schools
- Flyers to homeschooling organizations
- Flyers to churches and community organizations
- Visits to schools and booktalks for classes

All of these publicity efforts are useful, although they may not reach very far beyond families already committed to library activities. Specific groups such as non-English-speaking parents are often better reached through newspapers and radio stations targeted toward them.

Signing up children for the summer reading programs is an important step because the appeal of many programs depends on setting a target that can be reached and celebrated by the end of summer. Registration in the library is an obvious first step, but allowing registration on the library website makes it easier for many families to participate. Children can also be registered at schools if the librarian can make arrangements with principals and teachers. For younger children, parents must do the actual registration, and this can be handled through daycare centers and preschools.

Recording progress is another important step. Traditionally, children have gone to the library and reported their reading to a librarian or clerk, who then noted the completion of a book. Most programs are more flexible now and may count progress as the number of pages read or the amount of time spent reading. Self-reporting, with or without the help of parents or other caregivers, is generally considered adequate. The reports of reading can be done either in person at the library or online through the library website. Purists may point out that children sometimes exaggerate their reading time or page count, but most libraries consider this a small price to pay for encouraging reading. Whether or not the statistics on reading are accurate, participation in the program probably does indicate some increase in the amount of summer reading.

Celebrating completion in a satisfying way is crucial to having a successful program. Holding a party at the library, preferably with both food and entertainment, is the traditional goal of many libraries. Local restaurants and groceries can sometimes be persuaded to donate food, or if the group is not too large, parents may supply refreshments. Entertainment by local clowns, storytellers, or magicians is available in most communities at reasonable cost. One of the biggest problems is finding a time when many families can attend, so most of these parties are held on a weekend toward the end of summer. Companies with a strong local connection can often be persuaded to donate prizes. Some of the most successful prizes have been

- paperback books,
- T-shirts,
- movie passes,
- fast-food gift certificates, and
- tickets to an athletic game or concert.

A certificate of completion and a small prize is usually given to every child who reads a specified number of books or reads for an agreed-upon target number of hours. A grand prize, such as a donor-sponsored family visit to a nearby amusement park, may be offered to the individual who reads the most books, although such a prize is likely to encourage the reading of short, easy books. Some librarians question the value of rewarding quantity of books read rather than encouraging children to stretch their abilities and read longer and more complex books.

INTEGRATING LIBRARY PROGRAMS WITH THE LARGER MEDIA WORLD

Many libraries reach large numbers of children through the traditional programs offered every year. What is a successful rate of penetration of the market? In other words, what proportion of children in your community should be involved in library programs? It's difficult to set a definite target, but unless there is some goal, it's impossible to judge how successful the library has been.

Whatever the number of children who participate, libraries are always hoping to include more. Retaining tried-and-true programs may serve many families, but in today's media world, there is no success without growth and change. Growing programs are the ones that get funding and community support. Families of preschool children may be satisfied with the same kind of storyhours they grew up with, but as children grow, they expect libraries to meet the changing trends they see around them. What are some of the ways libraries can move their services into the interactive age? Each category of program has opportunities, and the media children use give us clues.

After-School Programs

Music as a theme can be useful because as children grow from primary to intermediate grades in school, their interest in music tends to increase. Choosing music, whether it is country, hip-hop, or Latin, becomes a statement of larger cultural values, so the choice of music is important. Music clubs that give youngsters a chance to share music and talk about artists are attractive.

Video discussion groups can also be appealing. Children can watch videos based on children's books. In cooperation with local schools and universities, animation classes can be organized so that kids can see their own short films

Computer training sessions staffed by high school or college students can help young students learn to design their own webpages or to learn to use social media well. The older students gain credit for community service by staffing the programs.

Video gaming sessions are a popular program. These could be expanded into helping children learn to design their own video games.

Workshops on making videos or writing graphic novels can be very popular. A community volunteer may conduct the workshop, or a Friends of the Library group could pay for a teacher or other expert to help.

Homework Help

Most libraries already provide some form of homework help, but often only to students who come into the library. With the cooperation of Friends of the Library or parents' groups, volunteers could offer live chat sessions for students who log into the library website from home or from a mobile device.

Reference service for short queries can be given through online chat, email, or texting.

Summer Reading Programs

Many of the preparatory tasks for a summer reading program can be handled online, and this may increase the outreach of the program. Online services rarely replace face-to-face contact but can be helpful supplements. If much of the program is run online, a live celebration at the end becomes a special event where participants who may not have met each other can enjoy talking about their experience. Some programs are in dual format; for example in Pima County, Arizona, children can register and record progress either at their local library or online. Many features of the program can be handled either online or in person, including the following:

- Online registration is helpful because students can register from school or from home.
- Publicity on the library website and social media sites reaches people who may not visit the library often.
- Recording reading progress can be done online as well as in person at the library.

INTERACTIVITY IS THE KEY

The value of integrating newer technologies into services for school-age children doesn't come from the technology itself but from the opportunity it offers for interactive activities. Today's children want to be active learners and participate rather than be passive recipients of programs designed for them. Educators know that active learning tends to remain longer with the student than information simply presented by an adult, no matter how attractive the format. A book that is read and discussed with others through a reading club, blog, or wiki is likely to be remembered better than one merely read and returned to the library. The more opportunities we give young people for contributing to a program, the more likely they are to be enthusiastic about it. The constantly changing world of new technology is just another channel for encouraging children to become engaged in the exploration of library resources.

4

WHAT'S NEW FOR
TWEENS AND TEENS?

When do children become adolescents? The answers range over several years. It used to be that turning 13 marked the great event, but several writers have shifted the transition downward to 10. Earlier puberty may be part of the reason for the sudden changes occurring in many children as they enter the second decade of their lives. Marketing is probably even more important. "Tween" is a term coined to include the ages between 9 and 14, when many children begin to assert their interest in clothes and electronics, to insist on choosing their own entertainment and friends, and to reject many of the suggestions made to them by parents and other adults. Corporations have responded to the economic power of this age group by developing products for tweens that promise to increase their popularity with peers as well as provide entertainment. Books and activities previously enjoyed are rejected as "too babyish" or "boring" as tweens text on their cell phones and rush to watch the latest YouTube sensation.

DIGITAL NATIVES HEADING TOWARD ADULTHOOD

Technology is not the cause of the tween phenomenon, but in affluent American communities, it helps to create the age-restricted world in which they live. Even as tweens assert their independence, many of them are more geographically restricted than previous generations. Fears of kidnapping, even though seldom warranted, and of other dangers perceived in walking or bicycling, coupled with an inability to drive, mean that young teens are unable to mingle freely with their peers in spontaneous interactions. Much of their social life is conducted through electronic media. Connections with their families, friends, and the world at large are shaped anew every year by the availability of new tools. During the late 20th century, most American teens used these media:

- Books
- Telephone

- Television
- CDs
- Computers
- MP3 players

Each of these media has changed dramatically in the last 10 years.

- Books are still read, and some series books sweep through the population like magic, but increasingly the reading favorites are graphic novels.
- Landline telephones have been replaced by cell phones for most young people and often for their families.
- Television is ever-present in many homes and in many tweens' bedrooms. Television viewing is not necessarily a scheduled activity because DVRs can shift programs to suit viewers' convenience. Everyone in the family can watch a program at a different time on a TV set, a computer, or a mobile screen.
- CDs are disappearing, as are single-purpose MP3 players. Most music is downloaded, sometimes illegally, and listened to on computers or mobile devices.
- Desk computers have given way to laptops for homework and gaming, but for internet browsing and email, computers are being replaced by mobile devices.

Changing Interactions with Technology

The tweens of today have a new set of devices and activities, most of which not only give private pleasure but also connect them to a larger world. A report from the Kaiser Foundation in 2010 (Rideout, Foehr, and Roberts 2010) documents the explosion in ownership and use of personal media among 8- to 18-year-old youth.

Although several of these devices are owned by the majority of young people from ages 8 to 18, the percentage of individuals who own them increases with age.

	2004	2009
iPod/MP3 player	18%	76%
Cell phone	35%	66%
Handheld video game player	55%	59%
Laptop	12%	29%
Portable CD/tape player	61%	16%

Figure 4.1   Changes in personal media ownership over time.
Source: Rideout, Foehr, and Roberts (2010).

	Ages 8–10	Ages 11–14	Ages 15–18
iPod/MP3 player	61%	80%	83%
Cell phone	31%	69%	85%
Handheld game player	65%	69%	41%
Laptop	17%	27%	38%
Portable CD/tape player	9%	16%	20%

Figure 4.2   Changes in media ownership by age.
Source: Rideout, Foehr, and Roberts (2010)

Figure 4.2 demonstrates the sharp difference in media ownership that occurs for children as they move through school. Less than a third of the youngest group owns a cell phone, but by the time they reach their late teens, more than four out of five individuals do. One of the interesting differences between the cell phone and other devices listed is that a cell phone, although inexpensive to acquire, requires regular ongoing service payments. Over time, cell phones generally cost more to maintain than any of the other devices, including internet access for the laptop.

The most important, as well as the most versatile, of these personal devices is the cell phone because it performs so many functions, and cell phones are becoming more powerful month by month as more and more apps become available. Cell phones are popular with parents because they are a way to keep track of where their children are. Young people like them because of the versatility that makes it possible to carry on many activities with them:

- Social networking
- Texting
- Phoning
- Gaming
- Tweeting
- Reading
- Watching videos
- Surfing the web
- Finding locations and directions

Effects of Technology Changes

None of these new technologies has affected the basic developmental tasks that come with a new stage of life; instead, they modify the ways in which children interact with their environment. Mobile technology makes children, as well as adults, less dependent on location. In their homes, they are easily accessible to their friends, and outside the home, they are more easily locatable by their parents. These changes can give both parents and children a greater sense of control over their lives, although the amount of control is often illusory.

If the child, the family, and the community are functioning well, progress from sheltered family-based childhood to a more outward-turning adolescence can go smoothly. One of the reasons some tweens spend a great deal of time in the library is that it bridges the step from family to peer group. In the adult-approved, controlled world of the library, children can interact with their peers and develop the social skills they need for the rest of their lives. In this way, for specific groups of young adolescents, the library functions the same way a school band or athletic team might. Is this an appropriate purpose of library services to intermediate schoolchildren? Professionals do not always agree.

Tweens and teenagers are among the most talked about and least well served of library patrons. Librarians work hard to encourage them to come into libraries and then complain when they spend their library time in noisy, messy groups. It is difficult to plan programs for them because they often reject activities they view as imposed by adults. Yet asking for leadership from a group of young teens can easily raise unrealistic expectations, which are often overturned by the difficulty most youngsters have following through on tasks and focusing on long-range goals. The 10- to 14-year-old group still needs adult guidance and help with organization as they learn how to manage their activities. Determining the right mix can be difficult.

WHO NEEDS THE LIBRARY?

Throughout their first 10 years of life, children tend to welcome reading books and going to the library, but as they enter the tween years, many turn away. Public libraries may have a faithful group of pre- and early-teen users who find a home in the library, but many of their peers come to believe they no longer need libraries. The reasons fall into several categories.

No Time for the Library

In surveys of schoolchildren, the major reason given for not going to the public library is lack of time. When children enter middle school, typically in fifth or sixth grade, they usually switch to a format in which they have a different teacher for each subject. Homework is assigned by each teacher, and the total amount generally exceeds what is expected in earlier grades.

At the same age when they face this transition, students find that organized sports and other activities become more important and time-consuming. Many students in affluent neighborhoods have four or five afternoons a week scheduled for sports activities and classes. Other lessons and sports take up many weekend hours. Whether these kinds of planned activities are good or bad for the average child is hotly debated on blogs and in parent groups, but the scheduling is a reality for many children.

Many tweens are in the difficult position of being old enough not to need babysitting every minute they are not under parental supervision, but being too young to drive and get around the community by themselves. Public transportation to local libraries and community sites is generally available only in large cities. This means that children are often confined to their homes or a small neighborhood area after school. Without a parent or babysitter to offer transportation, the library becomes inaccessible.

No Interest in the Library

Turning away from books and libraries is seen as a tragedy by librarians and many other adults, but nonetheless, it's a familiar path. As youngsters become capable of choosing for themselves how they will spend their leisure time, some of them decide books have little to offer. In this, they join many adults in our society. Once the thrilling but difficult task of learning to read has been mastered, what need is there to waste time on idle reading? Reading is necessary for homework, just as it will be for most jobs later on, but as a pastime, it pales beside the pleasures of playing sports, watching television, playing video games, texting friends, or checking on Facebook.

Learning to read is a communal experience in a classroom, and reading aloud to others and listening to someone read are shared activities. When youngsters turn to reading on their own, they may find it rather lonely. Unless their friends also become interested in reading and talking about books, the act of reading can cut off communication. This runs counter to the need of children to interact with their peers and gain acceptance from others. Most adult-approved activities for children, from sports teams to choirs, are group activities. It's no wonder many children don't take to the solitary pleasure of reading.

No Need for Bricks and Mortar

Even children who enjoy reading may not feel the need for a library. The big-box stores where many families spend several hours every week offer displays of popular paperback books for all ages. The prices are low, and although these stores do not offer a wide range of books, they frequently have enough to keep most tweens satisfied. For people who want a wider selection, the large bookstores found in most shopping malls carry hundreds of enticing series books and graphic novels along with a small group of medal winners and literary classics. Besides the books, these bookstores usually have comfortable chairs, cafes, and plenty of floor space. Many sponsor author visits and parties to mark the publication of particularly big sellers. And if there is no bookstore nearby, thousands of books are available for purchase online. With so many opportunities to buy inexpensive books in the normal routine of family life, why make a special trip to the library?

Children in elementary school need information to complete their homework assignments, but frequently they don't need the library. Much homework is based on textbooks or handouts from school. For topics that require more research, most children turn to the internet on their home computer. It's not that children, or their parents, are effective searchers, but the time spent on false leads and filtering through overwhelming numbers of hits may not be any greater than the time it takes to go to the library. Best of all, a child does not need any adult transportation to do research at home. Parents are relieved of the burden of evening drives to the library to track down a particular bit of information for an assignment due the next day. It's not surprising that both parents and children find this method of research more congenial than using the local library.

WHAT LIBRARIES ARE DOING FOR TWEENS AND TEENS

When any group of patrons stops coming to the library, or comes less often, librarians are apt to view this as a failure. Accustomed to the enthusiastic response from parents and children to preschool storyhours, librarians may take the absence of school-age children in the department as a personal failure. Frequently, the attitude from librarians and administrators is that every effort must be made to get bodies into the building, even though this may not be the best use of library resources. There is an argument to be made that evaluating a library by the number of people who cross the threshold may not be appropriate. There is further discussion of use of the library from outside the building in chapter 8.

Traditional Programs for Older Children

Many of the same kinds of programs mentioned in chapter 3 are provided for children through their tween and teen years, including the following:

- Homework help
- Summer reading programs
- Reading groups
- After-school programs

Homework help remains an important service as children enter the higher grades of school and their information needs become more complex. A third grader may require help in learning how to find basic information from a computer search, and the sixth or seventh grader will require sophisticated search strategy for some projects. Most libraries limit one-on-one homework help to specific time periods during the week because it is labor-intensive for librarians, and it is not easy to find volunteers who can handle it. As students grow older, face-to-face help in the library may be supplanted by online help. Many 10-year-olds are comfortable using a computer and interacting with others in a chat session or by email. Of course, much homework is done at times when the library building is closed, which may limit the use of online chat. Emails don't offer the instant response that many youngsters are used to and often don't serve to answer questions for an assignment due in the morning. These are difficult issues for the library to resolve.

The New York Public Library offers an online homework help program called Dial-A-Teacher, which uses a virtual whiteboard. Students log on and can ask a question or post a math problem. The teacher can choose to type a helpful suggestion, add a drawing, or identify a website that could provide information. This help is available four days a week during after-school hours (www.nypl.org/blog/2010/03/26/dial-teacher). Other libraries offer a range of homework help to students outside the library, some using a program called Tutor.com, others by providing telephone help from local staff.

Summer reading programs remain a mainstay of library services for all age groups. With the cooperation of schools, libraries can get a good response to registration and often reach large numbers of school-age children, although the numbers enrolling often drop when students enter middle school. As mentioned in chapter 3, summer reading programs are important for several reasons:

- Keep children from losing reading skills over the summer
- Give the library a high profile in the community
- Develop a connection with the library that may continue during the school year

Summer reading programs designed for tweens and teens operate very much like the ones for younger children, although many libraries use different themes for children of different ages.

Reading groups and after-school programs are less often provided for older children than for the younger ones. By the time children enter middle school, they often have access to sports or other programs through schools and church groups, which occupy most of their afternoons. Library programs may be viewed as too childish because they are associated with the preschool storyhours. Librarians have to work very hard to keep this group interested in library activities.

The Big Move—Leaving the Children's Department

Almost every public library has a children's department, either a separate room or a designated space within the adult library. The children's department is usually designed to serve children from birth to the age of 12 or 14. What happens to children when they become too old to want children's services is a question that has vexed librarians for many years. Some adults believe teenagers should move on to using the standard adult services, whereas others advocate offering a young adult or teenage department to make the transition easier. The Young Adult Services Division of ALA (YALSA) is an active and fast-growing professional group that recommends strong support services for young people who are no longer children but not quite adults either.

PATTERNS OF TEEN COLLECTIONS IN LIBRARIES

When focusing on the physical library, the provision of services for this age group becomes a logistical problem. During the middle years of the 20th century, when young adult services were being established, many libraries set up a special room for teenagers and a specialized staff to serve them. The Cleveland Public Library, for example, had its Robert Louis Stevenson Room. Later, as library architecture became more open, many libraries favored an arrangement to facilitate movement from one department to another. Often, a collection of mostly fiction books for young adults was placed near the children's room to encourage tweens to start choosing from these shelves. The reference services for young people were gradually shifted to the adult department or to school libraries, which became more numerous in most jurisdictions during this period.

Choices for the Location of Teen Collections

1. Separate department in a designated area or room with a specialized staff. For many years, this was viewed as the ideal, but it has the drawback of isolating teens from other users, and some teens may be lost to the library when they grow too old for the teen section.

2. Area of children's room with materials for young adults (YA) maintained by children's department staff. Having the YA section linked to the children's department encourages the transition for younger readers into reading longer and more challenging books, but as children develop more confidence, they may lose interest. They sometimes consider the children's department too young and inappropriate for them but still not feel ready to use adult services.

3. Area of adult department for YA materials maintained by adult department staff. In many libraries, this arrangement works well, but sometimes, adults resent having to share space with young people, some of whom may be noisy and rude. Success depends mainly on the attitudes of adult library patrons as well as the staff, who have to smooth relations between the groups.

4. No separate area for YA materials but designated staff to serve teen patrons. Many libraries use this pattern, inter-shelving some teenage material with the adult collection and some with children's. Problems may arise when patrons do not recognize that one or more of the library staff has a special interest in serving teens. The success of this arrangement often depends on the abilities and choices of individual staff members.

5. No special provision made for YA collection or staff. Titles duplicated in children's and adults departments when appropriate. With the prevalence of budget cutbacks in recent years, many libraries have neglected YA services. Some young people move easily into adult services, but it is likely that more will stop using the library under these conditions.

No matter what the physical arrangement of the library, most libraries still notice a drop in library use as children grow into their second decade. Children eight and nine years old may use the young adults' fiction collection, causing the teens, who are the target audience, to decide it is too young for them. Combined with a shift to digital media, which often makes books less appealing, and the availability of school libraries, these factors spell the end of public library use for many teenagers.

Keeping Teenagers in the Loop

Teen websites. Many public libraries have made effective use of websites to encourage teens to visit the public library. Two examples are shown in Figures 4.3 and 4.4.

The Carnegie Library of Pittsburgh uses a locker graphic to suggest school activities on one side of the homepage and a pleasure-reading suggestion with a new book review on the other side, creating an inviting entry for the department.

The Los Angeles Public Library uses a bulletin board theme to suggest the range of tween and teen interests. The untidy mix of elements gives a teen-friendly, active look, suggesting some of the many overlapping interests of young people. Quick sketches of individuals in action and handwritten notes on torn-off pieces of notebook paper give the feel of being in touch with teens, although in reality many teens would be more likely to make a quick electronic reminder on their cell phone than to use paper.

Programs for teens. Gaming in libraries has become one of the most popular programs for tweens and teens. The programs are typically presented in the evening and can be structured to meet the needs of the community. A variety of formats can be used for these programs:

Figure 4.3 Carnegie Public Library teen webpage. *Source:* http://www.clpgh.org/teens.

Figure 4.4 Los Angeles Public Library teen webpage. *Source:* http://www.lapl.org/ya/.

INFORMAL GAME NIGHT

For younger tweens, this can be a family program in which parents and children work together at a video game. Usually, the atmosphere is informal, and competition is minimized. The idea is to have a friendly, family atmosphere. Children enjoy instructing their parents on the finer points of the game. Parents who may be unfamiliar with the library are introduced to it in a nonthreatening, enjoyable atmosphere. Some libraries find that board games work just as well as video games for these programs.

VIDEO GAME TOURNAMENTS

As young people get older and want to be more independent, they may prefer video game tournaments to family game nights. In this format, the group is split into four-person teams that compete against one another. In libraries that have wireless internet access, individuals can bring their own laptops. In libraries without wireless facility, some individuals may choose to work with mobile devices. Other libraries will have enough computers to meet the needs of the group. It is important to have a person in charge who can troubleshoot any difficulties with the machines and also keep the event going in a friendly atmosphere. Recording the scores of each team and awarding prizes to members of the winning team help make the event a success. Kids also like to have the scores publicized on a blog or the library website.

Gaming nights have been successful in many libraries, but there have been questions raised about whether they do much to increase awareness of library collections and services. Often, they attract people who use the library regularly, but sometimes they are valued more by groups of teens who are not library users. Encouraging the transition from visiting the library only for specific activities to becoming a library user may be difficult. Library staff may encourage students to stay at the library after the gaming time is over by serving refreshments, but this too can cause problems with library policies and maintenance staff. Book displays featuring books related to gaming or based on video game characters can increase interest in reading.

OTHER PROGRAMS FOR TWEENS AND TEENS

Other more traditional types of library programs continue to be popular in many libraries. Often these programs are offered with the help of volunteers or community groups.

Crafts are a traditional library-sponsored activity for the tween-to-teen group, and in many communities, they have had a recent surge in popularity. Knitting is no long a gender-limited craft, so boys and girls together enjoy learning to make simple clothing items. Jewelry making, T-shirt design, and cooking (if the library has appropriate kitchen equipment) are also popular. Photography clubs attract patrons in many communities where young people have access to good equipment. The promise of making a video that can be posted on YouTube is appealing to many young people and can provide good publicity for the library. One of the advantages of craft programs is that often volunteers from the community can provide the leadership, while the library provides the space, publicity, and organization of members. Working with another community group is also a way to strengthen ties between the library and others in the community.

Author or illustrator visits can bring a bonanza of publicity and interest, but these take considerable time and often cost money. Most libraries don't have the resources to handle more than one or two in a year unless local authors are willing to donate time. Some libraries find that cooperating with a local bookstore, which provides in-store publicity, can improve visibility and attendance. In exchange for the cooperation, the bookstore handles sales of the author or illustrator's books. Going virtual with celebrity visits is also an option, and many authors and illustrators are experienced in presenting their work online and chatting with a distant audience. As with all technology-dependent programs, it is best to rehearse the presentation equipment and to work with experienced staff. Sometimes students from media programs in local high schools or community colleges are willing to volunteer to help the library. Many of them are experienced and resourceful.

Anime clubs are another popular type of program. Many colleges and individual artists offer these workshops for children and teens as well as adults. If an interested library staff member or community volunteer is available, the workshop can be extended into an Anime Club to offer participants a chance to practice their skills. Usually, a fee is required to pay for instruction and supplies, and this may pose a problem for some libraries. Funding could be sought from Friends of the Library or another community group or local government if there is a high demand for the program in a community of limited resources.

Getting Input from Tweens and Teens

Most libraries have found that programs for older children and teens are better attended and supported when the target audience has input in planning. As children enter their teenage years, they want and need to take control of their own activities, try out their ideas, and work with their peers to make things happen.

Teen Advisory Groups

An organized group or advisory board of teens can help to ensure the growth and success of teen programs and also provides a bonus for the library by giving fresh ideas and easy publicity to library programs. Organizing and maintaining a teen advisory group takes time and requires effort, but the rewards are great, including the following:

- Providing a built-in audience for programs
- Spreading information about the library to a wider audience
- Maintaining contact with children who have outgrown storyhours and other programs
- Bringing in young people who have not been library users
- Influencing parents and community members who may be unaware of library activities

As the teen board becomes more active, the library will be able to plan programs with a wider appeal than those suggested only by library staff. Popular media and communication tastes change so quickly that it is almost impossible for staff members to keep up with the latest trends. If the teen group can be made representative of the whole community and not just a small group of perennial library users, they can widen the library's area of service.

Teen advisory groups also provide input into decisions about collection development. The best way to find out what young people want to read is to ask them. The best way to discover how they are using communication tools and what they value about them is to watch and listen. A well-run advisory group can be one of the library's most valuable assets.

The San Francisco (California) Public Library sums up the function of a teen advisory group by posting this description of their Teen Advisory Council:

WHAT IS THE TEEN ADVISORY COUNCIL?

The San Francisco Public Library Teen Advisory Council is a group of San Francisco high schoolers who want to make the public library a better place for teens. We meet every month at the main library to plan library events such as the teen summer read program, and other teen-related programs. We make ideas happen.

We aim to make the library more visible for teenagers, so that they will know about the great free resources we have right here in our city. Each council member is responsible for advertising library programs in our area of the city. We talk to other students about what the library has to offer.

We also want teens to participate in library decisions. We meet with library administrators to let them know what improvements the library can make to invite all teens inside the doors.

When you join the Teen Advisory Council, you agree to learn leadership skills such as sharing your opinions, negotiating with other teens, speaking in public (if you want!), contacting other agencies, applying for special funding (money!!). As teenagers, we can give our input on how money provided by the Friends and Foundation of San Francisco Public Library should be spent. In the past, we've successfully started S.A.T. prep workshops, a talent show, film programs, and a DJ skills workshop.

As a Council member, you also get to participate in fun events like the summer reading party and author visits.

If you want your voice to be heard, and you care about the public library, or you want to improve the library, apply for the Teen Advisory Council today!!

From http://sfpl.org/teen_blog/?page_id=379.

Setting Up an Advisory Group

Having clear goals for an advisory group will help to avoid disappointment for the library staff and for teens. Be sure the staff knows and can articulate the rationale for the group before you start recruiting. There are a number of issues to decide:

Large or limited membership? Do you want to encourage as many people as possible to join the group? This can bring in many suggestions for programs and services, so librarians can choose which ones to implement. A large membership may increase participation in library programs and increased circulation. Having a large membership can also lead to many changes, with groups of students joining and dropping out together at the end of a school year or perhaps when seasons change and other activities are available. On the other hand, a small group, perhaps elected by teenage patrons, is likely to have more continuity and take responsibility for specific activities such as sending a representative to the library board meeting or volunteering to help with weekly programs for younger children.

How much power does an advisory group have? Is the library committed to buying materials or organizing programs suggested by the group if they are feasible, or are suggestions from the group treated the same as any other patron request? Will the advisory group have input into setting roles for the library? Will they be consulted about changes to the décor or the technology available in the teen area? Will the teen group represent the library on any public occasions such as municipal board meetings or high school visits? If teens agree to serve on a board, they should be aware of their roles and responsibilities.

What will the costs be for maintaining the board? Although the teen advisory board should not be a major expense to the library, there will be some incidental expenses. At any meeting of teenagers, food is welcomed and must be paid for. Some funds should be budgeted for purchases of materials recommended by the board. Some sort of prize or recognition at the end of a year would also be appropriate.

Recruiting and Training Members

Because there is likely to be a high turnover in teen groups, recruiting and training are ongoing. Following are some ways of finding new members:

- Advertisements and flyers within the library in highly visible places—the photocopy machine, water fountain, computer stations, bathrooms, check-out machines
- Notices on the library's website, especially the teen page, and the Facebook page
- Taglines added to the email signature of library staff when responding to reference or other questions
- Announcements at library programs, including adult programs
- Special displays in teen area
- Talking to library patrons, library shelvers, and their friends
- Announcements sent to local schools for posting on the school library website
- Offers to schools to use the program as a community service credit
- Ads in local newspapers or community newsletters

Keeping the Advisory Group Inclusive

Tweens and teens tend to form small groups, or cliques, which can be unfriendly to young people they perceive as outsiders. For any library group, we want to include representation from all segments of the community. It is important to encourage participation from all ethnic and social groups represented in the community, and this is often best done through the schools. If applicants for the group are coming mainly from longtime library patrons, try to contact teachers who might be able to suggest other candidates. Because library use is sometimes higher among girls than boys, try to keep a gender balance by asking teachers or coaches to suggest names. Sometimes it is a challenge for adults to overcome the clannishness of teens, but being an inclusive group will strengthen the credibility of the advisory board and also of the library.

Meetings

Most teen advisory groups meet at the library monthly either after school or in the early evening. Often, a library staff member chairs the meeting, although sometimes one of the teen members may handle this. Agendas are often set by the library staff in consultation with members of the advisory group. The balance between staff and teens depends on many factors, one being the average age of the members. In some libraries, the groups consist of young teens who welcome strong support and leadership from staff. If an older group forms, members may prefer to handle more of the group management themselves. The growth of interactive technology has changed the way meetings are held in many organizations.

RESPONSIBILITIES TO EMERGING ADULTS

As mentioned in the first chapter, children's departments foster children's developments through the most crucial years of their lives. Emerging literacy is one of the first themes, as libraries encourage children as they learn to talk and eventually to read. By the time teenagers move beyond the age group served by children's departments, they are emerging adults, ready to take on the complex intellectual and social tasks of higher education and adult life. In the next two chapters, we look at the specific literacy skills that libraries foster in young people to help them reach that point.

SECTION II

LITERACIES FOR THE 21ST CENTURY

5

CHANGING LITERACIES
FOR THE 21ST CENTURY

Libraries and literacy have always been closely entwined. Literacy is the key to unlocking library resources, but more than that, it is now seen as an essential right for every individual. The Nobel Prize–winning economist Amartya Sen has written,

> Illiteracy and innumeracy are forms of insecurity in themselves. Not to be able to read or write or count or communicate is itself a tremendous deprivation. And if a person is thus reduced by illiteracy and innumeracy, we can not only see that the person is insecure to whom something terrible could happen, but more immediately, that to him or her something terrible has actually happened. (2003, p. 22)

American libraries may take their role in promoting literacy for granted, but in a time of expanding media, the concepts of literacy are changing dramatically. As librarians, we need to look at the place of literacy in modern society and the forces that are affecting the ways young people interact with ideas and information in a global setting. Children need to master a whole range of skills to become truly literate today.

DEFINITIONS OF LITERACY

Literacy can be defined in many ways. The United Nations has taken literacy as one of its major themes, and over the years, the definition of exactly what literacy is has changed several times. One widely accepted definition that was current for several decades was the one adopted by UNESCO in 1978: "a functionally literate person is someone able to carry out all the activities which require literacy, reading, writing, and calculating for the good functioning and development of his or her group or community and for his or her own development." Changes in technology and in society have prompted several recent changes in this definition. One proposed operational definition formulated in June 2003 states,

Literacy is the ability to identify, understand, interpret, create, communicate and compute using printed and written materials associated with varying contexts. Literacy involves a continuum of learning enabling individuals to achieve their goals, to develop their knowledge and potential and to participate fully in their community and wider society. (UNESCO 2004)

These definitions acknowledge that literacy is not a trait that a person either has or lacks, but rather is a range of skills. The degree of literacy needed by a small farmer in rural India would be quite different from that needed by a computer technician in Mumbai. In addition to the traditional abilities of reading and writing, functional literacy includes the concept of numeracy, the ability to handle numbers and perform mathematical tasks.

Although this definition of literacy acknowledges the importance of being able to understand information in a variety of contexts, it does not specifically note that changing technology also influences literacy. Many researchers and commentators have recognized that literacy is not a single ability but a range of skills. Terminology varies, but the generally accepted branches of literacy include at least the following:

- Print literacy—the ability to read and write written materials; the basic form of literacy that makes many of the others possible
- Information literacy—the ability to locate and use information effectively
- Visual literacy—the ability to create and understand images and media
- Media literacy—the ability to access, evaluate, and create messages in a variety of media
- Multicultural literacy—the ability to compare and appreciate differences in culture

IMPORTANCE OF PRINT LITERACY

Literacy is important both to the individual and to society, and the need to develop near-universal literacy has become an increasingly important goal in our current technology-driven information society. The modern world demands a literate workforce to perform the tasks necessary for modern industry. Literacy, therefore, is generally viewed as of great economic value both to nations and to individuals. UNESCO strongly supports this view and has used it as the basis for supporting literacy programs throughout the world. Literacy for all is the goal toward which the organization has been aiming throughout its history because that is seen as a basic human right:

> In addition to being a right in itself, literacy allows the pursuit of other human rights. It confers a wide set of benefits and strengthens the capabilities of individuals, families and communities to access health, educational, economic, political and cultural opportunities. (UNESCO 2005)

Yet, the report continues, on average, less than 60 percent of the total adult population in sub-Saharan Africa and less than 63 percent of adults in the Arab world can read and write with understanding. All over the world, literacy rates for women are lower than those for men.

Despite tremendous progress made over the past 55 years, universal literacy remains a major challenge for both developing and developed countries in terms of commitment and action. There are over 800 million illiterate adults in today's world—a figure projected to remain unchanged in 2015 if current trends continue unabated. (UNESCO 2004, p. 3)

Although it is undoubtedly true that developed countries with strong economies generally have a high rate of literacy, it is not clear that improvements in literacy rates are closely tied to an improving economy. Certainly, a low literacy rate is associated with high poverty rates and a poor economy, but the relationships among these factors is complex. One scholar has put forth the unpopular opinion that "the great danger, one which twentieth-century education on all levels shares with literacy models, is the simple presumption that economic development in particular depends directly on investment in and high rates of productivity from systems of formal education" (Graff 1995, p. 331). Graff argues against what he calls the myths of literacy and cautions against expecting too much from alphabetic literacy without considering the importance of other skills, abilities, competencies, and knowledge.

One problem is that the value of literacy is often viewed in the context of a society rather than an individual, yet the burden of attaining literacy always falls on the individual. An African may spend long hours learning to read and write texts in an indigenous language. When the individual reaches an acceptable level of performance, the achievement is counted as a gain for literacy. If he or she does not have access to written materials that will help in finding a job, or increasing productivity as a farmer or merchant, the literacy is little gain for the individual. Without sufficient texts to educate, amuse, or enlighten the newly literate person, there is no incentive for maintaining or increasing literacy. If all available texts are in one of the major languages of the world, there may be no advantage to an individual in being literate in an indigenous language. In discussing the value of literacy, attention should be focused on advantages to the individual as well as to society. This is one reason for the importance of libraries, one of the few institutions that offer literacy materials to individuals. Libraries focus on individuals and are able to keep literacy skills alive by offering materials that appeal to each person who uses the service rather than trying to offer them to a group. Increasingly, libraries will have to focus also on providing more than just print sources to increase literacy because other literacies are needed in today's world.

Social Advantages of Print Literacy

A highly literate society is often glibly accepted as a desirable goal, but it is worth looking at some of the specific advantages that literacy brings:

- Complex societies would be impossible without literacy. Literacy enables communication between individuals separated in space and in time. Oral societies rely on the ability of one person to speak to another, or to many other people.
- Without writing (at least until the development of electronic recording media), it was impossible to speak to people who were not alive at the same time as the speaker. Once writing was invented, it became possible to record stories and facts

for future generations. If information stored in digital format does not remain accessible, it will lose all value.

- Literacy makes it possible to pass on information to people scattered over a large area without relying on messengers. In the absence of stable texts, either written or recorded in another format, there is always a possibility that the messenger might pass on an incorrect message.
- Writing supports memory, making it possible for people to record and analyze large amounts of information. Although the ability to write may have lessened people's ability to memorize, the volume of written material in any culture far exceeds the amount that any one human being could memorize. A literate culture can maintain a far larger store of information than an oral culture can.
- Writing makes language stable and tangible so that ideas can be examined closely. Laws that are committed to writing gain a depersonalized authority. Justice in a literate society depends less on the personality and knowledge of a judge and more on accepted laws. In this way, literacy can contribute to social control.

Oral societies tend to be small and fragmented. When writing is introduced, an administrative infrastructure can be developed to hold together cultural units that may be geographically separated. In China, for example, writing served as a unifying bond for millions of people over a large geographic area. The Chinese were able to accomplish this even though they never had anything like universal literacy. There were only a small number of literate individuals within Chinese society, but they were able to formulate regulations and communicate across geographic boundaries so that a cohesive society evolved.

MAJOR CAUSES OF ILLITERACY WORLDWIDE

1. *Poverty.* Lack of resources within the family unit is one of the greatest predictors of illiteracy. Children and adults who must spend most of their time searching for food and shelter do not have the time or incentive to learn to read. According to the UNESCO website, "one in five adults is still not literate and two-thirds of them are women while 67.4 million children are out of school" (UNESCO 2011).
2. *Gender.* During almost all of history, entry into the group of literate people was limited to males. Education of women was not considered important because the valued work of the world was carried on by men. Women needed only enough literacy to work efficiently at the tasks assigned them by their fathers or husbands. Even today throughout much of the world, illiteracy is much greater among women than among men. The education of boys is valued more highly than the education of women. The UNESCO statistics for literacy indicate that 64 percent of illiterate adults in the world are women. Although Western countries have seen an increase in the proportion of females obtaining education during the past 50 years, this trend is not maintained throughout the world. The increasing number of fundamentalist Islamic governments has led to a sharp decrease in the availability of education for girls in countries such as Iran and Afghanistan during the last 20 years. Whether this trend will continue or not remains to be seen.

Other Factors Limiting the Development of Print Literacy

Small Language Communities

The number of different languages in the world has been estimated to be 6,909. Of these, 389 languages (or nearly 6 percent) have at least 1 million speakers and account for 94 percent of the world's population. The remaining 94 percent of languages are spoken by only 6 percent of the world's people (Ethnologue Languages of the World 2011). Most languages spoken in the world have no written form, although they are the first language of small groups of people. The value of providing writing for all of these languages can be questioned. Individuals living in a society where all communication is oral are not likely to feel deprived if they cannot read and write. Historically, one of the major reasons for devising a written form for small languages has been to enable speakers of those languages to read religious materials, usually Christian writings. In fact, the desire to promote people's access to devotional materials has been one of the most important forces in the development of literacy in many countries. Now that digital visual and audio recordings are available, minority languages can be preserved even though no written form exists.

Although the desire to maintain all living languages is widespread, the movement raises many political issues. Every child needs a home language to communicate with others in her family, to talk to herself, to listen to the stories of grandparents. (The home language is often called the "mother tongue," but this phrase can be misleading, suggesting that the mother's native language is always the preferred language of an individual.) In a period of rapid change, however, every child also needs a language to communicate with the outside world. Economic opportunity, freedom of movement, and the ability to take a job depend on the knowledge of a language spoken by an economically viable community.

When a language dies, a portion of the world's culture disappears. It is important to remember, however, that languages are not static; they naturally change and merge as groups extend their territory and intermingle with people speaking other languages. Some languages disappear while others spread over a wider area. Linguists and ethnologists have occasionally been viewed as trying to maintain a small language group as a museum rather than a living and changing social community.

Language Policy in Multilanguage Countries

Japan is one of the few countries in the world where almost everyone has the same home language. Many other countries have one language that is the home language of a large majority of the population—England, France, Germany, and Spain are examples of this, but each one of these countries has a sizable minority of residents whose home language is not the majority language. In the United States, an increasing number of people have a home language that is not the majority language. In Europe and North America, this occurs primarily through immigration, although some European countries include geographically distinct minority groups such as the Basque. In North and South America, Australia, and much of Asia, indigenous people with a distinctive language coexist within the majority-language community. Most of these countries have one official language for education and government, although some have two.

The situation is very different in much of Africa and parts of Asia, where many different languages are used by groups within the same country. Many of these are former colonial countries where the language of the colonial power served to link different tribal groups within one country. The breakdown of the colonial governments led to a reevaluation of language policy.

The language used for government is most commonly the language of power in any community. Citizens who do not speak or understand the language of government are at a disadvantage in gaining power and prestige. Higher education is almost always first provided in the language used for government. Those who do not speak this language have no opportunity to obtain important positions in the country

In African and some Asian countries, European colonialists were always a small minority of the population, but their languages were dominant. When the African countries became free, starting in the 1960s, some chose to keep the colonial language as the official language in order to unify the country. Others chose one or more indigenous languages as official languages. These decisions have had a profound influence on economic and cultural development. Many groups of indigenous people speak a variety of languages, especially in the countries of Africa, and much recent language policy has been devised to satisfy the needs of these people. In several African countries, there is no language that is spoken by a majority of the population. This makes the establishment of an official language or languages extremely difficult.

Availability of Written Materials

Literacy once attained is not always maintained. Unless newly literate people have texts to read, they are likely to lose their literacy. Small languages typically do not have many texts with which to practice reading. What reading material exists may be unsuitable either in content or in format for the newly literate to read. The costs of books and other written materials are often prohibitive. Many of the newly literate are poor people. If they have to make a choice between food and books, almost inevitably they will choose food.

There are a number of ways that individuals in former colonial countries have tried to provide suitable materials. One example is Kwela Books, established in South Africa in 1994 to offer opportunities for African writers who were ignored during the apartheid years. When it was started, it announced a competition for manuscripts. Writers could write in any of the 11 official languages of South Africa. All titles selected for publication would be produced in at least three languages. Eighty-six manuscripts were submitted, but only nine of these were in indigenous languages. Over the years, Kwela's publishing goals have changed, and all of its recently published books are either in either English or Afrikaans.

The market for indigenous-language books in South Africa and many other African countries is largely limited to schools and libraries. Individuals prefer English because it is the language of aspiration. When the same children's story was made available in Xhosa and English in a library, the children chose English as a matter of pride. Parents usually prefer to have their children read English books because they believe these give the children access to jobs and advancement (Mpe 1999).

Successful literacy programs have attempted to overcome this problem of lack of materials. When Botswana established its Village Reading Rooms to increase the level of literacy, lack of materials was soon recognized as a problem.

> In the field, however, both librarians and literacy teachers were becoming increasingly concerned about the relevance and benefit of their services to the people. The librarians were very aware of the limited number of books available in local languages and on topics of interest to the ordinary citizen. This lack of suitable literature was due to the small size of the publishing industry. . . . In a country where most publications were coming from outside, the literacy teachers were faced with a desperate situation of having no suitable material to sustain the literate environment that they were trying to create (Mulindwa 2000, p. 3).

Through cooperative programs, the National Library Service has been able to publish about 40 pamphlets a year in Setswana, one of the largest language groups in Botswana. These pamphlets give the new literates reading materials with which to sustain their literacy.

Changing Alphabets

Literacy is difficult in some languages because of the variety of alphabets used in writing. One example of the result of this is Inuktituk, the language spoken by the Inuit of Alaska, Northern Canada, Greenland, and some areas in Russia. Although there are regional differences in the spoken language, many speakers of Inuktituk can understand the language spoken by other Inuit groups. The written language, however, presents problems because of different alphabets. During the 19th century, missionaries in Canada adapted the Cree writing system for Inuktitut script. "The Inuktitut script has been widely used by the Inuit in most of Canada except in Labrador, but in Alaska and Greenland a Roman-based system is used" (Rogers 2005, p. 253). More Inuktituk-language books are published in Greenland than anywhere else, but Canadian Inuit cannot read them because of the different alphabets; they are therefore cut off from a great deal of shared culture even though oral communication between the two groups is easy. There have been suggestions that literacy maintenance would be much easier if all Inuktitut material used the Roman system, but this solution has been rejected by the Inuit of Canada because the use of the Cree-derived syllabary symbolizes for them their unique identity. Fortunately, many of the materials can now be made available in recorded oral or electronic formats that can be presented in a variety of ways.

The countries of the former Soviet Union also struggled with changes in alphabetic system after the fall of the Soviet Union. The Soviet government had provided Cyrillic forms for many local languages in order to encourage the transferability of literacy. Many of these formats have changed since 1991. In Azerbaijan, for example, changes in alphabet systems have made literacy difficult. The biggest difficulty in promoting reading in Azerbaijan is that the alphabet has been changed four times during the last century:

- In 1923, a Latin alphabet was adopted and existed along with Arabic until 1929.

- In 1929, Arabic was completely banned.

- In 1939, a Latin alphabet was changed to Cyrillic.
- In 1991, a Cyrillic alphabet was changed back to Latin.

"None of those alphabet changes has truly been successful in terms of enabling younger generations to access the knowledge acquired by its older members in society. Each time the alphabet was changed, the younger generation was left orphaned, alone on its own to scrounge around as best it could to search of the repository of national, cultural, and historical knowledge" (Blair 2000, pp. 10–12).

For many Azeris, the return to Latin since 1991 has created difficulties. They have never learned to read and write in Latin script, whereas their children and grandchildren are already used to Latin. The problem is that very few books are published in Latin script these days, even though it is an official alphabet. Most of the library collections in Azerbaijan are in Russian language or Azeri Cyrillic. Even though the Azerbaijani language was declared as the state language in Azerbaijan's constitution in 1995, Russian language books are still in heavy use because of lack of appropriate resources in Azeri (Nazarov, 2000).

Ineffective Education

Statistics about literacy are generally based on figures for years of schooling. Such figures can be misleading because some individuals lose literacy even after several years of attending school. And there is some evidence that primary schooling may be ineffective in providing literacy skills. The quality of primary education varies dramatically from one country to another. In many countries, schools are inadequately funded and may lack such necessities as electricity, adequate desks and chairs, toilets, and heat. Inadequate preparation of teachers has been suggested as a reason for failure in many schools. An emphasis on rote learning and a tendency to teach for testing rather than for learning has been blamed.

Natural and Human Disasters

When disasters such as drought, storms, war, and disease strike a region, primary education is one of the first casualties. School attendance is a precarious privilege for many children in developing countries. When difficulties of any kind arise, children are kept from school. Teachers are also vulnerable because they are low-paid workers who can be called on for other duties when the need arises. Delays in education are often never recovered. If a year or two passes before schooling is reestablished, many students may miss the opportunity for literacy entirely.

Following are some recent examples of disrupted schooling in various populations:

- Wars and civil disturbances in the Great Lakes area of Africa have led to massive internal migration and loss of schooling.
- The AIDS epidemic in sub-Saharan Africa has created many orphans who must now stay at home to care for younger children instead of going to school. AIDS has also led to the deaths of many teachers, leaving schools without instructors.
- Refugee populations from Afghanistan, Iraq, Sierra Leone, Somalia, and Sudan have very little access to education.

- Earthquakes and flooding in Haiti, Pakistan, and Central America have shut down schools for extended periods and slowed the educational progress of thousands of children.

WHERE DO LIBRARIES FIT IN?

In considering the obstacles to achieving literacy for all, it is clear that librarians and educators do not have the power to solve all of the problems. For librarians in North America, many of the difficulties of encouraging literacy may seem to have little relevance to their work, but we live in a global economy, and more and more areas in the United States find themselves coping with the limited literacy of new immigrants. An understanding of the background of library patrons and their families is a vital part of planning library services. There is no such thing as a typical American child, and libraries have a responsibility to be knowledgeable about the various backgrounds and needs of their patrons and potential patrons.

Providing Print Materials for Non-English Speakers

Schools have the major responsibility for teaching children to read, but libraries are vital links in maintaining and increasing literacy. Providing materials in the home language of major linguistic groups in the community is an important responsibility. Many large library systems have extensive collections of non-English-language materials. Books are usually rotated to each branch as needed, but collections are often small.

Online books and other print materials can be a major resource for providing books in small languages. The International Children's Digital Library (http://en.childrenslibrary.org/) is one of the most useful sources for attractive, well-edited books in many languages for children. Foreign-language websites also have listings of online books for children.

Eliminating Social Barriers to Literacy

Poverty is the greatest cause of illiteracy worldwide, and America is no exception. Children growing up in the pockets of poverty in this country present the greatest challenge to schools and libraries. Children whose parents are unemployed or struggling to maintain a home by working several jobs often miss many days of school. Without home encouragement, children may lose their chance to become literate or may not retain the education they receive. Most children lose some of their reading ability over the long summer vacation, and children in poverty who may not have parents to take them to the library or buy print material suffer the most. Many libraries have traditionally offered summer reading programs, but often, most of the participants come from secure middle-class families, and the children who could benefit the most do not participate. Libraries should make an effort to offer programs planned to be attractive and convenient for children and families living in poverty. Rural poverty often isolates children during the summer months, and bookmobiles, local television programs, or online contacts may offer some of these children the advantages that libraries have to offer. Online summer reading programs can be very effective in rural communities.

Working with Other Community Groups

Most communities have a variety of groups with an interest in promoting literacy and education. Educators and librarians have a great deal of firsthand experience with literacy projects; their experience and knowledge can be of great value if they become more proactive in influencing policy decisions. Librarians' professional concerns extend to gender differences in education, policies to encourage indigenous publication, and the provision of recreational as well as informational reading for all. Working with other organizations strengthens libraries and serves children.

VISUAL AND MEDIA LITERACY

Print literacy has been the traditional focus of libraries, but in recent years, there has been more emphasis on the importance of visual literacy and media literacy. The term "visual literacy" was first used in 1969 by John Debus, founder of the International Visual Literacy Association (http://www.ivla.org/org_what_vis_lit.htm). Many definitions have been offered over the years, but they all center on the idea of the ability to recognize and understand images from print, pictures, graphs, maps, or digital formats. Every parent has observed the careful attention young children pay to pictures and has seen the expression on a child's face when she recognizes what an image represents. A large part of the charm of picture books lies in the recognition of images on paper, whether presented as drawings, collages, paintings, or photographs. In recent years, many wordless picture books have been published, and one of the appeals of these is following a story told solely in images. With the presence of television, computer screens, and mobile devices in most children's lives, the interpretation of visual images has become of major importance.

Understanding Pictures in Print

Parents sometimes assume that, in contrast to reading text, children need no special education in visual literacy, but educators have recognized a number of problems children experience in understanding what images reveal. To the casual observer, the pictures in picture books seem simple and straightforward. We know that young children cannot read words, but we often expect them to understand pictures effortlessly. In fact, children have to learn the visual conventions of a picture before they can understand what they see.

Young children understand objects as a whole. A baby learns about a ball by seeing its color and shape, by observing the way it rolls, by feeling its texture, by hearing the sound as it hits the floor, and often by putting it into her mouth to taste and smell. The knowledge of a ball involves all five senses. The red disk on the page of a board book bears little resemblance to an actual ball, but young children learn that the red disk represents a ball. A ball on the page of a book is an abstraction of the idea of a ball. Recent research on young children reports that even very young children recognize a picture, but they often find it difficult to understand the difference between an image and reality. Nine-month-old babies who were shown color photos of individual objects almost all reached out to grab the object as if they could pick it up from the page. There are reports that some children try to put their foot into a picture of a shoe.

It takes several years for children to understand the nature of pictures. John H. Flavell of Stanford University says that until about the age of four, many children think that if a picture of a bowl of popcorn is turned upside down, the popcorn will fall out (DeLoache 2005). If children have difficulty in understanding pictures of familiar objects, we need to be aware of how much more complex the pictures of animals, people, and complicated objects that children find in picture books are. While young children are learning the conventions artists use in picture books, there are a number of elements that may cause confusion:

- *Perspective.* Objects at a distance are not really smaller than those in the forefront of a picture. It is our familiarity with perspective that enables us to recognize that a ship in the distance is actually larger than the person standing on a beach.
- *Details that extend beyond the frame of the page.* When half of the body of a cat is shown on a page, the child may think the animal has been injured.
- *Comparative size of objects.* Pictures that are the same size do not always indicate the objects portrayed are the same size. On one page, a dog takes up the whole page; on the next, a truck may be shown taking up just as much space. Neither the dog nor the truck is really four inches high, and they are not the same size. A child has to learn that turning a page can introduce a new scale of measurement.
- *Continuity of pictures in a story.* Only gradually does a very young child learn that the boy throwing a ball on the first page of a book has thrown it to the dog shown chasing the ball on the next page.

Children who are read to when they are very young learn the conventions of visual representation in books. Giving children time to examine the pictures in a book, often over and over again, is important. The illustrations in picture books for older children, ages three and up, are often very complex. They introduce fantasy elements and pictorial sophistication that offer children an exciting introduction to art.

Print Images in Different Formats

During the second half of the 20th century, there was an effort to capture the experience of picture books on film. Some filmmakers consider the two media incompatible; Ingmar Bergman has written, "Film has nothing to do with literature: the character and substance of the two art forms are usually in conflict" (Bergman 1966, p. xvii). Nonetheless, lovers of literature have been fascinated by the idea of turning books into visual formats, and picture books seemed to be an easy place to start. One company that tried to transform book to film without losing any of the qualities of the print book was Weston Woods. This company's experience provides a good example of the differences between print and film media.

Morton Schindel, founder of Weston Woods, started his venture with the announced intention of producing picture books on film so that they would be clearly visible to all children in a group. He developed the iconographic filming technique to reproduce the book accurately. The camera moved across each printed page, picking out and highlighting various details in the picture. Watching this kind of film, the viewer has the impression that the film is a projected version of the book.

Despite the fidelity of the filming, the film version offers a child an experience different in several ways from the book. Instead of having the story told in a sequence of pages that can be turned slowly or quickly, the film unrolls at a steady pace not controlled by the child. Instead of scanning each page as a child does when looking at a book to discover the important elements and deciding which area to examine most closely, when viewing a film the child has his or her attention directed to pre-selected highlights each of which is shown in a particular order. No matter how carefully this is done, it takes some of the selection task out of the hands of the child and gives it to the filmmaker. Similarly, if the film is narrated, the experience is likely to be subtly different than if an individual in the presence of the child reads the text aloud.

As Weston Woods continued to make films based on picture books, it moved even further away from the book experience. Instead of the iconographic style, it began using an animated style with additional pictures added to the book illustrations to make the pace livelier. Instead of a narrator reading the text of the book, actors with different voices read the dialog portions of the text, and music was added to heighten the emotion expressed in pictures. Although Weston Woods has continued to produce films based on picture books and has never gone as far as other production companies in adding new story lines or live action, its films are now clearly a video using film techniques rather than a "picture book projected." In 1999, Weston Woods was purchased by Scholastic and is now a division of that company.

Children watching a film version of a book are learning a kind of literacy different from the print literacy of books. They learn how to keep up with a standard pace, they learn that a looming face is usually just a close view of a figure seen earlier, and they learn that a dissolve can mean the end of a segment. All these may seem obvious but are actually learned through experience.

Understanding Digital Images

Most young people in America spend more time watching digital images on television or the internet than they do looking at images in books. Much of the material they view on television, and to a lesser extent online, is designed for adults and takes little account of its audience of children. Many families have a television set turned on all day long and into the evening, so children get used to having strangers on a screen performing actions unconnected with life in the house. As noted earlier in this book, research indicates that few parents monitor what their school-age children are watching on television.

There are many layers of reality on contemporary television shows. Some dramas and comedies are scripted narratives that follow the arc of a fictional story; other shows are "reality" series that are structured so loosely that they appear to be unscripted, although many of them are heavily directed to produce certain actions; game shows and interview shows have people introduced by their own names and participating in ostensibly unscripted, although well-planned ways to entertain the audience. Then there are animated shows, both the children's cartoons and the primetime features, which require children to learn another set of skills to interpret.

Interspersed with regular shows are advertisements, taking up a great deal of air time. According to the A.C. Nielsen Company (http://www.csun.edu/science/

health/docs/tv&health.html#tv_stats), the average child sees 20,000 30-second television commercials a year. The amount of television watched has been well documented, but the question of how this viewing affects children is more difficult to answer. Some early studies indicated that even at the age of four, many children could tell the difference between ads and programming (Donohue, Henke, and Donohue 1980). The question that remains is whether children understand the intent of advertising and why it is used on television. A recent study of 8- to 12-year-old children in Europe suggests that younger children do not have a clear understanding of why ads appear and who benefits from them. Some 6-year-olds thought ads were necessary to give television actors a rest, or to allow the audience a break. By the age of 10 or 11, children understood that the purpose of advertisements is to sell things to people. Many of them still enjoyed the ads, but a few had negative attitudes and thought some ads exaggerated the quality of products (Andronikidis and Lambrianidou 2010).

There is far less research about the extent to which children grasp the way online messages are sent and the intentions of the sender, but it is likely that young children find many of the ads and websites they encounter online even harder to understand than television content. Jakob Nielsen, who has studied the way children use internet sites, comments,

> The most notable finding in our study was that **children click website advertisements.** Unfortunately, they often do so by mistake, thinking ads are just one more site element. In nine years of testing adults, we can count on the fingers of two hands the total number of times they've clicked website advertising. But kids click banners. They **cannot yet distinguish between content and advertising.** On the contrary, to kids, ads are just one more content source. If a banner contains a popular character or something that looks like a cool game, they'll click it. (Nielsen, 2002)

In educational settings, the concept of media literacy includes the ability to read, view, or listen to messages in any format and to sift through what the message means. The Center for Media Literacy (http://www.medialit.org/reading_room/rr2def.php) uses an expanded definition:

> It [media literacy] provides a framework to access, analyze, evaluate and create messages in a variety of forms—from print to video to the Internet. Media literacy builds an understanding of the role of media in society as well as essential skills of inquiry and self-expression necessary for citizens of a democracy.

The distinction between visual literacy and media literacy is somewhat fuzzy, but that is to be expected because of the convergence of many forms of media. Young children begin by learning to recognize visual images presented to them in various formats, and only gradually do they come to understand that these images are made by individuals who have created them for particular purposes. They may be intended to help children understand the world, as in many books and films, or to persuade children to take an action or behave in certain ways. Media literacy is a lifelong effort; even adults often have difficulty understanding the purposes of some messages and the ways in which they are crafted. An entire industry has been created to develop messages that persuade people to accept specific cultural or

Medium	Primary target age	Year developed	Primary marketing aims of sender	Importance
Radio	Preschool through adult	1920s	Entertainment Selling products	Secondary tool
Television	Preschool through adult	1950s	Entertainment Selling products	Most important selling tool
Magazines	School-age through adult	20th century	Informing Entertaining Selling products	Decreasing importance
Billboards	School-age through adult	1920s	Selling products and ideas	Secondary tool
Product placement	Teenage through adult	1970s in movies and television	Selling brands	Unobtrusive influence
Internet	School-age through adult	1995	Informing, persuading, selling	Growing in importance
Social media	Teenage and young adult	2005	Communication Selling products and brands	Growing in importance
Viral videos	School-age through adult	2005	Informing Selling products, candidates, ideas	Growing in mportance

Figure 5.1 Persuasive messages aimed at children.

political ideas. Some of the tools used to persuade children and adults to make decisions and purchase products are shown in Figure 5.1.

Libraries help children develop media literacy when they make available a variety of media to children and especially when they encourage children to discuss and to use them. When children talk about the products of various media—books, television shows, movies, or videos—they tend to think more deeply about the messages that are being sent. When they become aware that other people may interpret a story or a show differently than they do, they realize that messages are not always clear and simple.

Using media to create their own messages is also a part of increasing media literacy. Librarians can give children a chance to write blog reviews of books or produce video book trailers. These help children learn how to craft persuasive and appealing messages, while their audience is learning how to interpret them. The more interactive the library programs are, the easier it is for children to become knowledgeable about media. Libraries are not only storehouses of media products in many formats, but centers of creating, observing, and interpreting various media messages.

MULTICULTURAL LITERACY

Multicultural literacy has been defined as "the ability to acknowledge, compare, contrast, and appreciate commonalities and differences in cultural behaviors, beliefs and values, within and between cultures" (Cordes 2009, p. 3). This concept has been valued in American public libraries since the mid-20th century. As the number of Americans with non-European ethnic backgrounds continues to grow, libraries as well as schools and other cultural institutions have focused on presenting material drawn from different cultural backgrounds. Publishers started seeking authors and illustrators from diverse backgrounds, especially African Americans and Latino groups. A great deal of publicity is given to the statistics about the growth of the minority ethnic populations in many states. The idea of a "majority minority population" in states such as California has led to many discussions about what this will mean, although no real answers are available, and the impact may be less than expected.

Building a More Multicultural Library Collection

The first big push for diversity in books started during the 1960s and coincided with a decade of prosperity during which both publishing and libraries expanded. The civil rights movement in the United States raised many questions about why racial minorities, especially African Americans, were seldom represented in children's books. Many publishers began to seek out books with minority characters, and those written by African Americans were especially prized. Many important authors such as Virginia Hamilton and Julius Lester began writing children's books at this time, and libraries bought their books eagerly.

Gradually, other groups, such as Native Americans and Hispanics, started demanding representation in children's books. This movement has made children's literature collections far more representative of the cultural mix in classrooms and communities than they once were. There are still, however, many groups who are infrequently shown in children's books and films. These include some of the major immigrant groups in the country, who have come from China, the Philippines, India, Pakistan, Vietnam, and other countries. In addition, there are distinctive religious and cultural groups such as Jewish Americans and Muslim Americans who are not widely represented in books for children. A look at the Newbery Medal Award winners for the last decade gives some indication of which groups are most often represented in honored books.

NEWBERY MEDAL WINNERS

2010 *When You Reach Me* by Rebecca Stead (white children in New York)
2009 *The Graveyard Book* by Neil Gaiman (nonrealistic creatures)

2008. *Good Masters! Sweet Ladies! Voices from a Medieval Village* by Laura Amy Schlitz (European children in historical setting)

2007 *The Higher Power of Lucky* by Susan Patron (white children in California)

2006 *Criss Cross* by Lynne Rae Perkins (white children and teens)

2005 *Kira-Kira* by Cynthia Kadohata (Japanese American)

2004 *The Tale of Despereaux: Being the Story of a Mouse, a Princess, Some Soup, and a Spool of Thread* by Kate Di Camillo (European children and animals)

2003 *Crispin: The Cross of Lead* by Avi (European children in historical setting)

2002 *A Single Shard* by Linda Sue Park (Korean children in historical setting)

2001 *A Year Down Yonder* by Richard Peck (white children in America)

The prevalence of multicultural book collections has increased dramatically during the past 50 years. Most large library systems have both multilingual and multicultural collections. The multilanguage collections may rotate through branches to have the greatest possible impact despite budgetary restrictions. Smaller library systems usually try to provide a multicultural collection, even though some of them can offer only a token collection of books in languages other than English.

Some librarians believe that multicultural books are primarily useful to children whose own background mirrors that of the characters in the book, but it is very important that all children have access to books with characters of different ethnic backgrounds. Children living in communities where a majority of residents have European backgrounds are done a disservice if they do not have a chance to read about representatives of many different ethnic and cultural groups. Libraries should avoid having only token representation of minority children in a book or in the collection as a whole.

Technology and Multicultural Literacy

The internet is a global tool that can offer many resources for bringing people together if the librarian takes the time to search out websites and resources suitable for children. Depending on the age of the children, some of the library's programs could extend beyond the local community. Examples include the following:

• Online reading groups can include children from different neighborhoods within the library's jurisdiction. This is especially useful when different ethnic groups live in clearly defined areas. An occasional face-to-face meeting is helpful, but much interaction can be online.

• If a community has a Sister City program, children can prepare video reviews of favorite books, post them on YouTube, and then invite children in their sister city to respond. Many children throughout the world enjoy practicing English by exchanging messages with American children.

- Podcasts of children's book or video discussions can be exchanged among librarians in different communities or different countries.
- The library's Facebook or other social media page can "friend" children from a library in another country and exchange ideas and photos.

As new technology is developed and children begin to use other equipment, librarians will no doubt think of other possibilities. There are many ways for libraries to encourage multicultural literacy; all that is required is a strong commitment to the goal. The children of today are growing up in a global society and will need to be able to understand and interact with people who have far different backgrounds than their own. Libraries can provide materials and services that open the world for children.

6

———◆◆◆———

DEVELOPING INFORMATION
LITERACY

In the previous chapter, we examined the importance of literacy both to the individual and to society. Although print literacy is the foundation on which societies have been built, individuals today need a wide range of abilities that are not limited to decoding print on paper. Literacy today and in the future means not only the ability to read and understand print, but also the ability to understand and communicate in other formats with many other people. Children in the 21st century will need several kinds of literacy.

- Print literacy—the ability to read and write written materials, the basic form of literacy that makes many of the others possible
- Information literacy—the ability to locate and use information effectively
- Visual literacy—the ability to create and understand images and media
- Media literacy—the ability to access, evaluate, and create messages in a variety of media
- Multicultural literacy—the ability to compare and appreciate differences in culture

HOW DO MULTIPLE LITERACIES AFFECT
INFORMATION SEEKING?

Librarians may be overwhelmed by the idea of having to help children achieve all these different literacies. It is a daunting task, especially when we consider how difficult it is just to keep up with the print books that appear every year. Librarians have for many years played a crucial part in introducing children to books and encouraging literacy. Selecting books and making them available to children takes up most of the workday in libraries. Now there are many other formats and modes of interaction that are being required. How will the planning and workload of librarians change to meet these new requirements?

Changes in Collections

The components of multiple literacies have led to several important changes in library collections. Most obvious is the inclusion of different formats. Print was the first and most traditional format; next came audiovisual materials of various sorts; and more recently, we have digital materials. All of these are now an important part of public and school library collections. Children need to be able to access and integrate ideas from various types of materials, and this leads many librarians to believe that materials should be grouped not by form but by content. Format is an artificial barrier if we expect children to use all types of media with equal ease and skill. Technology makes it easier to integrate different formats, but librarians still have to think through the most effective ways to do this in their specific situation.

The need for multicultural literacy requires a somewhat different approach than the integration of formats. The need to seek out materials that represent different cultures and add them to a library collection cuts across all formats. Print, audiovisual, and digital materials come from all parts of the world and from many different cultures. Librarians today need to ensure that their patrons have access to the art, culture, and ideas of people who do not live in the local community or even the same country.

No one who has visited a children's library in recent years needs to be told that many different types of materials are now included in the collection, but many libraries have a long way to go to offer truly integrated collections and services. The difference between accepting various formats in the library (recorded music, DVDs, computer programs) and developing the library into an integrated facility encouraging multimodal literacies is a crucial one. Although most libraries have integrated their catalogs so that all materials are listed together, many still have collections divided by format. Audiovisual materials may even be housed in a separate room or section, which suggests they offer a different category of knowledge. In practice, most young users do not decide on the format they want until they have located materials on the subject that interests them.

Changes in Options for Searching

Consider the way in which a tech-savvy young person might search for information for a school assignment on a favorite sport. This fifth-grade student has chosen the topic "World Cup" for a class presentation. He goes to find materials on the topic and then he makes a series of choices:

1. He can check the library catalog to see what materials the library has listed. This is likely to lead to a list of the books and cataloged audiovisual materials on the library's shelves.
2. He can ask the librarian in the children's department for help, and quite likely the librarian will look in the catalog, identify a call number, and direct him to the section of books and other materials most likely to meet his needs. This sequence helps the child learn the technique of searching for information on a specific topic.
3. He can text or email a friend to ask whether he or she knows where to find the information.

4. He can use a computer or mobile device to do a Google search on the topic "World Cup," which leads to a list of websites, links to newspaper articles, images, and books dealing with the topic.
5. He can meet a friend in the library and ask for help in finding something on the topic. This is a more common approach than asking a librarian.
6. He can go home and ask an adult to help him find material. This is likely to lead to a Google search, although in some families the student might get an oral account of the World Cup games or teams.
7. He can log onto Facebook, Twitter, or another social media site to pose a question about the World Cup.

Only a few of these possibilities involve a librarian. This might lead us to wonder how important a part library collections play in the information seeking of young people. Although it is easy to understand why a young patron might choose any one of these methods, librarians know that information is likely to vary in quality as well as quantity. We'll go through them one by one:

1. A search of a traditional library catalog will yield only materials old enough to have been acquired and processed by the library. How serious a flaw this is varies by the topic, but for a search of "World Cup" conducted while the series is in process, the loss of information is significant.
2. Asking a librarian for help can yield very different results, but unless the individual librarian is personally knowledgeable about the subject, she is likely to limit the search to material in the catalog, thus limiting the results.
3. Asking a friend may produce some useful resources, but they are likely to be few in number and not necessarily reliable.
4. The Google search yields more sources of information than any of the other methods, but the quality of references is not monitored, and the sites suggested may be biased or incorrect. In addition, most searchers who are offered a long list of possible sources will choose the first two or three and ignore the rest.
5. Asking a friend in the library might be helpful, but the extent of the resources will probably be limited to browsing the shelves, which may yield nothing. It may also lead to another Google search.
6. Asking an adult at home or in the community may be helpful, if the individual is knowledgeable about the topic, but the average parent is likely to try a Google search and find the same disadvantages as the child.
7. Posting a question on Facebook or Twitter is unlikely to yield extensive information on a topic, although, with luck, it may lead to some useful resources. The chief problem with this strategy is that the information obtained is not evaluated and is likely to be both scanty and unreliable.

Merging Information from Different Formats

How can libraries manage their collections so as to make all forms of information available when needed? There probably isn't a perfect solution, but a great deal could be done if the librarian thinks about the way young people search for information. One obvious first step is to catalog all formats of materials in one integrated online catalog. Most libraries already do that for physical materials, but online resources are often omitted. Other suggestions include pathfinders on subjects frequently sought by young people and more extensive references in the catalog. Pathfinders define the topic and list both online and print materials; for examples, see the Internet Public Library (ICL 2) at http://www.ipl.org/div/ pf/entry/48473.. The catalog might include referrals to relevant databases, wikis, websites, and other digital materials on a particular subject.

The problem with these tools is that they are time-consuming to construct and must be frequently updated, or they lose their value. The pathfinders are useful for topics that are perennially needed by students, but many other topics individuals might want to find do not warrant the expenditure of a librarian's time to make a pathfinder. Integrating suggestions for databases into the catalog may be useful for many topics, but the same databases would likely be cited for many different topics, and children may find it difficult to search the database.

Library Instruction

Library instruction is another way for librarians to help children access the material they need, but in a public library, this is difficult to implement. Library instruction is most effective when it is given to an individual searching for a particular topic, but in most public libraries, the staff does not have time to give concentrated instruction to one child or a small group of children. Giving library instruction to a class of children takes much less time, but is also less likely to be remembered. Most children have difficulty applying techniques learned in one specific search to a different search. Library instruction is an important service in both school and public libraries, but the wealth of media available has made giving it more difficult than ever.

Many libraries still give library-based instruction classes, which are helpful, but the focus on using library materials does not realistically reflect the way most children conduct searches now and probably in the future. The weakness of the traditional library instruction class is that it is based in the library and uses the library as a model of an information center. Here, for example, is a typical library instruction class for a group of third- or fourth-grade children:

The teacher brings a class to the library to prepare for an assignment writing a report on an American state. The librarian has each child draw the name of one state from a prepared box of cards and shows the children how to access the library catalog and locate the entry for the state. Each child is responsible for finding a book giving some information about the state. When the book title is found and the information copied, the librarian gives a basic explanation of the Dewey Decimal System and helps each child locate the desired book using the call number. The next step is to ask each child to find a picture representing each state, and this gives the librarian a chance to explain the use of an image search and to demonstrate how to download an image to a Word file. The librarian also explains to the children that useful websites can be found through links on the library homepage. The final product of the lesson is a brief report on a state that can be printed and shared with the rest of the class.

This type of lesson will be useful to children as a guide to how they can find information on other topics for school assignments or for personal information needs. The weakness of the lesson as a tool for learning is that is assumes the child is going to start a search in the library and have access to library materials. The goal of the search is to introduce a method of searching the library to find resources; it is an introduction to the library rather than an introduction to finding information. The more libraries decouple themselves from buildings and become information services, the less realistic this kind of search is going to be.

Another weakness of this type of search is that it is heavily dependent on print sources and static pictures. Both of these may give excellent information, but many other facets of information on the topic may not be revealed if these are the only sources used. For an example, let's go back to the topic of the World Cup and look at how different formats give access to different types of information.

As librarians, we have tended to focus primarily on the library as the center of information-seeking activities, but in an electronically connected society, people are coming to expect information to be available from many different locations and in many different formats. Libraries need to prepare children to live in this information-saturated world and to find the facts they need whenever and wherever the need arises.

Format	Type of question answered	Information learned
Print	What teams were playing in the World Cup, and which ones won? Who were the players? What were the scores?	Names of teams and players; schedule of games; statistics of points scored
Video	What were the players like? How closely were the teams matched? What were the onlookers' reactions?	Pictures show the size and racial composition of team; tension of players' interactions; auditory and visual reactions of onlookers
Internet	How different were presentations in the home countries of various teams? What did sports experts say about games and players?	Wide range of viewpoints from several countries; both print and visual media; opinion and gossip about actions in the games
Social media	Did my friends watch the games? What did they think of them? Do they like the outcomes? What will they think of my comments?	Personal accounts of reactions to games—more meaningful to their peers than expert commentary; opportunity to tell others how they feel

Figure 6.1   Effects of format on information found.

FORMULATING QUESTIONS AND FINDING SOURCES

The American Association of School Librarians has developed a definition of information literacy, which includes the following:

- Defining the need for information
- Initiating the search strategy
- Locating the resources
- Accessing and comprehending the information
- Interpreting the information
- Communicating the information
- Evaluating the product and process (Eisenberg, Lowe, and Spitzer 2004, p. 20)

Formulating a Question

Defining the specific information need is often difficult for young people, who tend to express their need in terms of learning "about" a subject (for example, "I need to learn about snakes") rather than choosing a specific area of information. Starting on an information search with such a vague notion of what is needed can lead to quixotic results. A Google search can lead to a website such as a fact sheet from Kidzone (http://www.kidzone.ws/lw/snakes/index.htm), which is well organized to present the type of information needed by a child in the primary grades. On the other hand, the searcher could also link to a page that is aimed at academics and professional zoologists or one that advertises snakes as pets. The child needs some way of deciding which information is informative and relevant to her needs.

If the student chose to begin an online search by going to the YouTube website, a popular starting place for many students, the information available can be even more confusing. The first video that comes up in a search for rattlesnakes on YouTube is an account of a controversial rattlesnake roundup in Texas (Rattlesnake Roundup 2011). Although this video offers valid information about an aspect of rattlesnake life, it would not be an appropriate place to begin a search because it assumes some knowledge of the habits of rattlesnakes and attitudes toward them. The differing points of views given by characters in the film would be a good basis for class discussions for some students but would be more appropriate at the end of a project on rattlesnakes than as a starting point.

How can librarians help young library users to formulate questions that will guide them to search for the right sources of information? School librarians can organize classes that structure a search and lead children through the steps of formulating questions, deciding on sources, and recognizing answers when they are found. Many states and school districts have devised lesson plans for teaching children the basic concepts of information literacy. The American Association of School Librarians offers a great deal of information on the subject both in publications and in guidelines and standards available on its website (www.aasl.org).

Locating Sources

The classroom approach does not fit into most public library guidelines for service because in public libraries, children often come individually and in small groups from different classes and different schools. Reference interviews with individual children would be useful in helping them to work out useful questions to ask, but most experienced librarians know that children often seek information without going to a librarian for help. It seems that the best approach would be to use technology to prepare materials that children can access on their own and that can be quickly updated and edited as situations change.

Webpage Document

One of the easiest tools that a library could provide for children would be a page on the website that could be used as a template for finding information. The topics might include the following:

1. What is the subject you are looking for?
2. Is this a person, animal, country, or science topic?
3. What do you already know about the subject?
4. What information would you like to find?
5. Is this a topic that needs historical information or is it a current topic?

That page could link to a listing of library and online resources suitable for various types of topics—for example, encyclopedias for historical topics, image searches for pictorial information, and news websites for current events. These website pages could be printed out by a child and used as a guide for the information search.

Library Wiki

A wiki is a flexible tool that can be as elaborate as a website complete with images and videos or as simple as a group of documents filed together in one place. Many libraries are using wikis as a substitute for or a supplement to their website. For a children's department, the wiki offers the advantage of providing a space where librarians and patrons can share information about various topics. The same template of questions to ask in formulating reference queries that might be mounted on the website can also be posted on a wiki. This makes it easier for the librarian to edit and to suggest new resources for children seeking help on different types of topics. In addition, librarians can post lists of new books or other materials added to the library, provide sources or answers to current reference questions about hot topics, and share links to new websites or other online materials. Patrons can post questions and invite comments or questions from other library users, suggest resources outside the library, or add reviews of library materials. A wiki offers a model of collaborative work on solving information problems.

EVALUATING INFORMATION

By recommending and making available sources outside of the library's collection, librarians are helping children find more information on a wider range of topics than ever before, but also are increasing the risk of finding incorrect or questionable material. Because children are seeking information from so many different sources, both print and online, it is important for librarians to help them recognize reliable sources in all formats. It is not enough to say that print sources are generally more reliable than online sites, nor is that always true in a time when information becomes outdated quickly. For many science and social science topics, the information online is more current and correct than what is available in a library's print collection. Making value judgments based on format is bad library practice. There are basic concepts children should learn to help them in their information seeking, no matter what format the information takes or where it is obtained.

Recognizing a Reliable Source—Criteria for Various Formats

1. Library materials have been selected on the basis of reviews and expert knowledge, so books, magazines, and audiovisual materials in the library collection are generally reliable. This includes websites recommended on the library website. When current information is needed, however, it is important to check the date of the source and to search for the most recent data available.

2. Websites that come up in a Google or other online search vary in reliability. It is important to check several components of the website name.

   a. *Suffix.* The suffix at the end of the URL indicates the type of website or the country of origin. The most common suffixes for American sites are
   - *.com* for commercial sites;
   - *.edu* for educational institutions such as colleges and schools;
   - *.gov* for governmental agencies and bureaus;
   - *.net* for sites owned by an internet service provider;
   - *.org* for nonprofit organizations; and
   - suffixes that indicate the country of origin of the site—for example, *.de* for Germany, *.uk* for Great Britain, and *.jp* for Japan.

   Commercial sites are run by companies that are trying to sell products, so they are generally considered less reliable for information purposes than sites run by educational institutions, the government, or nonprofit organizations.

   b. *Organization responsible* for the site. The URL of a website often indicates which organization sponsors it—for example, www.redcross.org (American Red Cross). If the organization is well known and respected, information from its site is generally reliable. If the URL does not give enough information to identify the sponsor—for example, www.amnh.org (American Museum of Natural History)—the students should check the name of the organization on the homepage of the website or in the "About" file.

   c. *Purpose of site.* A reliable website usually includes an "About" file that states whether the site is designed to educate or inform people and what subject area it covers. The page should also include a list of the people who are responsible for the site, and for information sites, these should include experts in the subject field.

   d. *Date of last update.* Website information can be outdated and no longer reliable. Many websites have a note at the bottom of each page giving the date on which a page was last updated. This is an excellent practice, but not universally followed. Sometimes a copyright date at the bottom of the page indicates that the page is currently being tended; at other times, the date of update can be deduced from the currency of news items or other information given. If a website contains notices of meetings or events held several years earlier, it is an indication that any information found on it may be out-of-date.

3. *Blogs* are online sources that are difficult to evaluate for reliability. Blogs sponsored by well-known organizations such as the *New York Times* often tell the reader who contributes to the blog. The *Scientific American* magazine's blog Observations (http://www.scientificamerican.com/blog/observations/) lists the author of each blog post and their entries are considered reliable because they are sponsored by a respected magazine. Children's Hospital Boston features a blog on pediatric health (http://childrenshospitalblog.org/) and lists information about each reporter who contributes to the blog. These blogs with known authors, especially if they are sponsored by reputable organizations, are sources of reliable information. Unfortunately, many blogs available online are posted by people unknown to the casual reader. They may offer fascinating insights and ideas, but if used as a source of factual information, they should be checked against other sources known to be reliable.

4. *Wikis* are popular online sources that vary greatly in quality. Many wikis are run for the benefit of the sponsoring organization and can be accessed only by registered users. Children may have access to wikis at school or in organizations and should learn to check the credentials for the authors writing entries they wish to use. Just as in using blogs, it is best to have a second source for information found in a wiki.

5. *Twitter* (www.twitter.com) allows only brief comments of not more than 140 characters, which considerably limits the amount of information it offers, but participants often post links to websites, blogs, and other sources. Young people have not joined Twitter communities in large numbers, but it is possible this may change. Some librarians have difficulty believing that a flurry of brief sentences on a topic could be a credible source of information, but David Pogue, columnist for the *New York Times*, has elicited a number of good ideas for technical developments, such as new apps for smartphones, by putting out a call on Twitter (Pogue 2010). Another use for Twitter has been to aggregate information about ongoing events, which was an important function it performed during the disputed Iran election in 2009. Like many other online sources, the credibility of tweets (as the Twitter posts are called) depends on the authority of the author. Many government officials, authors, actors, and performers post frequently on Twitter, so it seems inevitable that it will eventually become a respected reference source.

6. *Social media* sites such as Facebook, MySpace, and others designed especially for children are other online sources familiar to young people. These are not generally considered useful reference sources. The bulk of the information available on a site such as Facebook deals with personal concerns as friends share news about parties and events. With more and more nonprofit

organizations mounting Facebook pages, however, there is an increasing proportion of solid factual information available. If the National Geographic Society announces on its Facebook page that a new comet-like planet has been discovered, as it did in July 2010, this can be accepted as reliable information. Because Facebook information is fleeting and disappears in the stream of posts, it is important to include the date of access to any reference to the material. The criteria, as always, is the authority of the reporting author or organization, so librarians and teachers should help young people sort out what is valuable on social media sites rather than disparaging them as valid sources. We lose credibility with young people when we don't take their choices seriously and examine them carefully.

This list includes some of the most popular sources of online information, but new sources will undoubtedly appear in the future. In teaching information literacy, it is important to give the basics for evaluation in terms flexible enough to be applicable to new formats as these appear. Learning how to use tools available in 2011, whether in print or online, will be a time-limited skill because seeking information in 2021 and beyond may require far different tools. The basic issues of knowing the source, understanding the purpose of the source, assessing the reliability of the creator, and understanding the importance of dating the information will still be important, no matter how much formats change.

COLLABORATIVE INFORMATION SEEKING

Collaboration in seeking information, designing products, and solving problems has become the norm in many information-age businesses. Today's school students will probably be working in a collaborative work environment when they embark on their careers. Some schools and some teachers assign the kind of group projects that encourage sharing of information. How can librarians create a collaborative atmosphere to foster this kind of work?

Collaborative Projects for Children

- Instead of a reading group, set up an exploring group to collect information about a topic of interest, from dinosaurs to space travel. The group could produce a wiki, a webpage, or a graphic book.
- Collaborate with a teacher or the youth leader of a community organization to document a history of the community or a portion of it, such as first settlements or a major disaster.
- If major renovations are being planned at the library, organize young volunteers to search for information about possible changes, and share their ideas with the community through a webpage, a blog, or a video.
- Organize a group of young musicians to document their songs using software such as Garage Band to produce recordings that could be shared with friends and family.

Some adult supervision would be needed to oversee these projects, but they would offer useful experiences for children and might attract patrons who would not participate in more conventional library programs. Many children, especially boys, lose interest in reading as they enter intermediate grades, but their literacy skills will be enhanced by computer-based reading and writing even if they avoid books. The library should be known as a center for information, not just for books.

Librarians Working on Collaborative Projects

Librarians can model collaborative information seeking and sharing by working on library-based collaborative projects. Webpages, blogs, wikis, and all of the web 2.0 tools can be social, collaborative tools, and in library departments they are usually group projects. When librarians create and use these tools, they are showing their patrons how they can be used and the way each individual adds to the value of a project. Allowing young people to help in working on these projects makes them partners in seeking and sharing information—an important skill for higher education and for employment.

Given that libraries in the future may put less emphasis on buildings and more on interactive diffused sharing of resources, each of these tools can be used by patrons either on-site or online. Their flexibility makes them invaluable resources for the digital generation.

Some Basics of Information Literacy

No matter how many new formats and tools may be introduced, libraries should remain a vital link in the task of improving information literacy if they remember the basic facts of information searching.

- Information comes in many formats.
- Defining information needs is a collaborative task.
- Librarians are guides to information in many formats—not just to library collections.
- Collaboration often increases the information available.

If librarians are flexible and forward-looking in helping children learn how to access and evaluate information, they will remain a vital force in community services for children. Children's libraries are gateways not just to children's literature, but to a whole world of information.

SECTION III

BUILDINGS FOR THE FUTURE

7

———◆◆———

CHANGING LIBRARY BUILDINGS TO MEET CHANGING NEEDS

The word *library* conjures up a picture of a building containing shelves of books and usually tables and chairs for people to sit and read. Children's departments may be visualized as light, colorful spaces with pictures and displays to add to the pleasures of reading. This picture is often quite accurate, but the design and décor of children's departments have changed over time, and there is no reason to think that even the most modern children's departments of today will remain as they are. The rapid changes in the way information and recreational materials are being disseminated suggests that libraries of the future may have to find new patterns to follow. In this chapter, we look at the way the essential concepts of a children's library has changed over the years and how they relate to society's view of what libraries should be and how children should interact with books and other media.

EVOLUTION OF CHILDREN'S LIBRARY DEPARTMENTS

Children's departments did not always find an easy welcome in American public libraries. A 1908 article in *Library Journal* expressed the opinion that children were getting too much attention from librarians and were displacing adults. "Let the schools educate the children, and, if you can, let the adult once more dominate the library practice. You will then have a well-balanced whole, free from over-emphasis on the child's side" (Mathews 1908, p. 138). By the 20th century, however, it was too late to turn back the tide of services to children, which had started in the 1880s and developed strength during the depression of the 1890s. This decade saw the growth of separate children's rooms in many urban libraries, often supported as a way to keep children off the streets and out of trouble (Jackson, Herling, and Josey 1976, pp. 22–23).

The physical design of the children's departments reflected the prevailing philosophy of library service, and as the 20th century advanced, changes in philosophy were reflected in the style of rooms offered to children. Alistair Black, in a presentation at the 2009 IFLA conference in Milan based on a coauthored paper (Black and Rankin 2009) described the historical evolution of library buildings over the

Figure 7.1   Children's section of public library c. 1922 (St. Paul MN). *Source:* www.stpaul. lib.mn.us/images/locations/saintanthony/Saint-anthony-park-1920s-lg.jpg.

20th century. His context was the British Isles, but the same trends were noticeable in North America and other European countries at the time. He identified three stages between 1900 and 1980.

1900–1920

Public libraries were designed as adjuncts to school and shelter from the idleness and bad influences of the street. Public libraries were often the only places open after school where children were welcomed. Early public library service, in both the United States and Great Britain, was based on the philosophy defined by Robert Leigh as "a belief in the virtue of the printed word, especially of the book, the reading of which is held to be good in itself, or from its reading flows that which is good" (1950, p. 16). The collection of books was the major defining feature of the library, and the children's department rooms themselves were similar to classrooms of the time. Furniture often consisted of rectangular tables with six or eight straight-backed chairs. Children were expected to sit quietly and read the books much as they would in school. Because libraries focused on reading, preschool children were not expected to use them.

1920–1940

As more progressive educational methods were introduced, the design of libraries as well as their materials changed. Public libraries were places children went voluntarily, in contrast to schools, so librarians began to plan children's departments that were more homelike. In place of the long, rectangular or round tables, more comfortable, softer upholstered furniture was introduced. Attractive pictures and growing plants were added to give the rooms a more homelike look. The idea was to make the library experience aesthetically pleasing while it provided intellectual growth. Younger, preschool children became a target of library programs, and parental involvement in libraries was encouraged. The school-like rules of silence were often relaxed.

1945–Present

After World War II, there was a burst of building of new libraries, which had halted during the war years. Library design was often modeled on the architectural plans of offices and schools being built at the time. Open-plan buildings with no clear demarcation between adult and children's spaces became fashionable in many communities. This was seen as a way to encourage easy transition from children's departments to adult sections. Earlier libraries had often rigidly separated children because adult patrons complained of the noise and disruption caused by youngsters. The postwar years brought a change of attitude toward children, and freer, less restrictive environments suited the times.

In the years since 1980, there have been many changes in library planning, although some libraries still work within the constraints of buildings erected many years ago. When children's services developed, many librarians believed they had a mission to protect children from popular culture, such as the series books and comic books available in stores. They wanted to provide an introduction to the best literature being written, and they set strict standards for collection development. During the second half of the 20th century, librarians became more receptive to popular culture and began to collect popular materials. This was reflected in décor, which was often planned to entice children by emphasizing interests developed

Figure 7.2 Public library children's room c. 1933 (Berkeley, CA). Photo by William Porter; Courtesy of Library of Congress.

Figure 7.3   Contemporary children's room (Redwood City, CA).

outside the library rather than to impose a librarian's standard of high culture on children. Instead of viewing children as blank slates to be nurtured and introduced to culture with library materials, librarians gradually accepted the idea that children arrive with definite preferences and interests derived from a variety of media. Libraries began to cater to children's interests in order to encourage them to become library users. As a result, more libraries began to copy the methods of businesses in marketing services to users.

FACTORS THAT INFLUENCE BUILDING DESIGN FOR CHILDREN

One concept that has remained in place as library attitudes have varied is the library as a specific location, a designated place, where children can find materials and services. Today, many libraries attempt to broaden their functions in order to meet many different needs of children, including the following:

- Provider of books and other materials—The oldest and still important service of almost all public library children's departments is to make books and related materials available.
- Schoolroom—Public libraries coordinate their work with schools by providing homework help for school-age children as well as books and other materials to

help children with their school-related projects. Some public libraries are housed in school buildings or are built in close proximity to them.

- Safe haven from the outside community—Libraries often function, sometimes without specifically planning for it, as after-school centers for children. Parents tell their children to spend time in the library because it is usually a safer place than the streets and play areas available.

- Surrogate home—As part of their role as a safe haven, libraries may become surrogate homes for children who spend long periods of time there. Parents and children together may also find that the materials and space available in children's departments of libraries make the building an extension of the home.

- Club or community center—The increasing provision of programs featuring gaming, video-making, hobby clubs, and other activities has given some libraries the function and feel of a community center for children.

- Venue for cultural programming—When funding is sufficient, most children's libraries schedule cultural events such as visits by authors, illustrators, or musicians to the library. This may be done in conjunction with the schools or another institution, but it is an important feature of library work in many communities.

- Provider of artistic and craft experiences—Many public libraries schedule workshops or classes where children can make holiday decorations, paint T-shirts, learn how to make a video, or paint pictures.

Whether any one of these purposes is of greater importance than others is an often-debated topic. Many people would say that providing books is the primary function of a library and that other functions are frills, but this can be a difficult case to argue. Many of the non-book-centered activities undertaken by libraries are designed to bring children into the library. The gaming nights are often planned in order to get children, especially boys who are not eager readers, into the library building, where they cannot escape seeing books and may be encouraged to try one. Are the programs marketing tools or necessary provisions for the needs of children?

NEW FORMS FOR LIBRARIES

The growth of new collaborative media has made possible the idea of a library that exists not as a building, but as a hub of information and entertainment accessible from many locations. There has been some discussion of libraries without books, stocked completely with digital resources stored outside the building. These concepts sound strange to most members of the public but are often discussed in library circles. What might be gained and what lost if a community moved toward this model?

Digital Libraries for Children

The concept of a digital library was first seriously addressed by the Digital Library Initiative of the National Science Foundation in the mid-1990s. The years since then have seen a great increase in the amount of literature that is "born digital," both created and stored in digital form, and "digitized" material that was first produced in print format and then converted to digital. The Google Books project as well as several universities have scanned and made available many out-of-print materials found in academic libraries. These materials are now available and can be accessed through computers at home, schools, libraries or workplaces. By the early 21st century it became clear that all new literature, whether destined for magazines, books or other formats, exists before publication in digital format. More and more literature remains in this format and never appears in print.

The first decade of the 21st century saw the appearance of exclusively digital libraries. Most of these are designed for use by specialists in science or technology or by university researchers and students. Public libraries are still heavily book-oriented, although more and more of their content is now digital.

Children have not been completely left out of the move toward digital content. The International Children's Digital Library (ICDL), as described on its website, "is a research project funded primarily by the National Science Foundation (NSF), the Institute for Museum and Library Services (IMLS), and Microsoft Research to create a digital library of outstanding children's books from all over the world" (http://en.childrenslibrary.org).

The ICDL's mission is to make available to children a collection of books in at least 100 different languages. The library digitizes books published in many countries and makes the full text including illustrations easily accessible on its website. This initiative expands the resources of libraries that have minority-language speakers in their community. Books in the first language of minority children can serve as a bridge to move into an English-language environment.

The ICDL is designed not as a replacement for a library, but as a supplement. It offers materials unlikely to be available to many of the children who would enjoy using them. Even though the format is digital, every effort has been made to reproduce the experience of the print product, which is seen as the source of content. ICDL has not produced digital content itself, nor has it chosen materials that have not appeared in print format.

Another version of a digital library for children is the "For Kids" section of the Internet Public Library (ipl2, http://www.ipl.org/div/kidspace/). The Internet Public Library, started in 1995 at the University of Michigan in a graduate seminar at the School of Information and Library Studies, is designed to make digital information available to its users. It does not include books or printed pages, but provides links to a number of sites that provide information on various topics. This is the way it describes how it works:

ipl2 is a public service organization and a learning/teaching environment. To date, thousands of students and volunteer library and information science professionals have been involved in answering reference questions for our Ask an ipl2 Librarian service and in designing, building, creating and maintaining the ipl2's collections. It is through the efforts of these students and volunteers that the ipl2 continues to thrive to this day.

In January 2010, the website "ipl2: information you can trust" was launched, merging the collections of resources from the Internet Public Library (IPL) and the Librarians' Internet Index (LII) websites. The site is hosted by Drexel University's College of Information Science & Technology, and a consortium of colleges and universities with programs in information science are involved in developing and maintaining the ipl2.

The ipl2 clearly considers itself supplementary to libraries by providing a service to librarians and their patrons as well as other individuals. With the growing importance of online sources of information for homework and other reference needs, however, there could be circumstances in which ipl2 might substitute for a library. In a community without the resources to purchase reference books, the links collected in the Internet Public Library could supply enough information to satisfy the average high school student's homework needs, making a large book collection unnecessary.

Hybrid Libraries

Why do we have a library building? The first answer most people would give is "to house the books." A series of articles in the *New York Times* in February 2010 asked a number of educators, librarians, and other experts, "Do school libraries need books?" (Room for Debate Blog 2010). Most of the answers indicated that, for the time being at least, libraries will need both books and digital sources to meet the needs of students. A few respondents mentioned the necessity of having a librarian to mediate between the needs of the students and the available information. Liz Gray, a library director, wrote, "Just because there's a lot of information online does not mean that students know how to find it, nor is the freely available information always the best information or the right information." Author William Powers commented, "The idea that books are outdated is based on a common misconception: the belief that new technologies automatically render existing ones obsolete, as the automobile did with the buggy whip. However, this isn't always the case. Old technologies often handily survive the introduction of new ones, and sometimes become useful in entirely new ways." The consensus seemed to be that 10 years into the 21st century, both books and electronic sources are necessary for young people. But what of the future?

If all or the majority of books migrated online, would libraries still be needed? The development of electronic book readers such as the Kindle, Nook, and iPad has led to questions about whether paper books are needed by most readers. When the Kindle was introduced, its lack of illustrations and color led many people to think it would never be appropriate for children's books. The iPad and other more recent readers, however, can supply almost all the attributes of a printed book except for the actual paper. In addition, electronic books can offer enhancements that printed books cannot. The type font can be enlarged to serve readers with visual disabilities, and audio can supply a human voice reading the text. Both of these possibilities are helpful to many children. In addition, short video clips of actions or processes can add information difficult to convey solely in print.

At the present time, expense makes e-readers out of the reach of most children even in the United States and other developed countries. We should remember that libraries were formed to make print accessible to more children when books were an expensive format. The economic purpose of libraries is to reduce the cost of written content to the individual user by combining costs for a large group. It's not clear how this model could be applied to ebook readers, but it is undoubtedly true that the cost of these readers will drop sharply in the next few years or decades. The cost of paper and the ecological cost of destroying trees to make paper may push the shift to digital formats.

Most children's departments today function as hybrid libraries, with various levels of emphasis on the print and nonprint sources. Quite a few have changed very little over the past 25 years and function chiefly as book environments with electronic sources limited to an online catalog. There is a continuum of integration evident in libraries today.

Traditional Book–Centered Department

This type of children's department is primarily a collection of books. In some small libraries, the children's materials are housed in a corner of the adult room, and all of the electronic services, including the online catalogs and computers to access databases, are in the adult section. If a full-time children's services librarian is available, her services are generally limited to book selection, interactions with parents and children about books, and programming such as storyhours and summer reading programs.

Book–Centered Library with Integrated Electronic Reference

In children's departments that have space for them, computers are often the first electronic equipment made available. If the children's department wants to serve school-age children, it generally needs to have access to the databases children are using in school libraries and classrooms. When patron-access computers were first introduced into libraries, they were often seen as add-ons that could be housed separately from books. Computer labs served first as word-processing centers and then were gradually transformed into facilities for the online searching of databases and the internet. In the early days of computer access, the machines were often restricted to adult users, but eventually, the demand became so great that teens and then younger children had to be allowed to use them.

The landscape is changing again as wireless connectivity becomes more available, and more computer use moves to laptops and mobile devices. Many teenagers and some younger children bring their own laptop or other device to the library. Some vendors now supply laptop vending machines so that patrons can borrow a laptop to use while they are in the library. The use of these machines requires a credit card, so an adult or older teen has to sign one out, but it is possible that further developments will make them more accessible to children.

Balanced Hybrid Collections

When computers were introduced in children's departments, they were primarily considered reference tools. For several years, reference materials were duplicated in print and online databases, although gradually, print reference books have become less affordable, and some libraries rarely purchase them for children. In many libraries, books, augmented by collections of CDs and DVDs, are expected to serve the recreational needs of the children, whereas online sources are for reference. This is gradually changing as wireless systems make online gaming and videos available on patrons' laptops and library computers. In an effort to keep up with this trend, some children's departments are bringing print and electronic materials together and using both to serve the recreational and reference needs of young people.

Blogs have become common in children's libraries, often used to review books or participate in summer reading programs. Sometimes, librarians do the blogging and encourage children to post comments; other times, the children themselves write blog entries.

The example in Figure 7.4 of a blog written by library staff shows the striking design that can be achieved with this format. Like most library blogs, its purpose appears to be introducing readers to the new books in the collection. It is an example of an electronic format being used in the service of the print format, so this is a true hybrid format, melding different methods of delivering content.

Blogs are organized to show the current content on top, so if a user does not visit the blog frequently, the content of older entries is difficult to find. Tags are used to enable searching by topic or author, but it is not clear how often children use tags to find information. A wiki format, used in some libraries, gives the user access to more stable information about books and other materials. One of the advantages of a wiki over a blog is that the information can be accessed from menus at the top or side of each page. This provides a permanent link to stable information such as requirements for getting a library card or schedules for holiday closings. Information about changing programs or new additions to the collection can be quickly updated by librarians or other staff members. There is no need for highly trained technicians. The trade-off for the ease of use and stability of wikis is that they generally do not offer the graphic possibilities available on webpages and blogs.

Both blogs and wikis can be written and edited by multiple authors, so it is possible to use them as interactive tools with young people. Most public libraries,

Figure 7.4   Public library children's blog (Springfield-Green County Library District, MO). *Source:* www.198.209.8.7/kidspace/.

however, choose to have librarian-written blogs and wikis. Patron comments are encouraged on many blogs, and individual children may submit reviews that will be incorporated into the blog. Generally, however, comments and blog posts are monitored by library staff to avoid the danger of offensive or inappropriate material being used. This is normal practice on many blogs, inside and outside of libraries, but it is worth remembering how firmly the reins of control are kept in the hands of adults. As social networks such as Facebook proliferate, there may be greater pressure from young people to take over more control of the interfaces provided by libraries. The ability to comment freely and to use colloquial language is highly prized in social media circles. Tight adult control of communication media may be difficult to maintain in an open interactive world.

Facebook pages have become almost standard for many public libraries and can be a good place to attract young people because so many of them visit Facebook several times a day. The Brooklyn Public Library offers a good example of effective use of a Facebook page. The distinctive logo welcomes viewers and encourages people to sign up as fans. The library keeps an up-to-date listing of events in each of the branches, with a link to the branch for additional information. Facebook has increasingly functioned as a pointer to websites, so entries there are a good way to increase website traffic. Here are some important suggestions for Facebook librarians to remember:

- Encourage staff and patrons to become fans and post comments.
- Mention the Facebook page in every school visit by librarians and encourage students to become fans.
- Post links to branch websites to encourage patrons to use online library services.
- Be sure to post events in a timely way—not too early, but a few days before the event. Because Facebook posts keep the most recent on top, outdated posts move down the page and are not visible without searching. For this reason, many libraries and other users do not worry about removing them.
- Post pictures and videos of events. Photo albums of special events remain available on the front page and can give the library useful publicity.

Once the library's Facebook page is established and has a number of fans, it can be a useful marketing tool. Staff members who assume responsibility for a Facebook page should keep up with the pages of other organizations and nonprofits. The tone generally used on Facebook is personal and informal, so don't post press releases to a Facebook page. Press releases are written in a style useful to newspapers and other media outlets, but Facebook postings should have a different format and tone. Postings should come from an individual and be written in an informal style, just as one friend would post for another. Linking with other pages can be helpful and gives a feeling of friendly cooperation. Even though the library is primarily going to mention its own events, a link to something going on in a nearby library or another community organization is helpful to readers and establishes a cooperative rather than competitive tone. Facebook pages are excellent places to thank volunteers and post pictures after an event. People who have helped at library events enjoy having an acknowledgement in a public space where friends and relatives are likely to see it.

Looking Ahead to a Seamless Blended Library

Most libraries began the 21st century with buildings rooted firmly in the 20th century. The digital revolution had improved traditional library services by making catalogs more easily accessible and flexible. As other features of the internet developed, reference tools gradually migrated online, and eventually, many reference services shifted to digital interactions. Children's departments developed and strengthened their websites and became more responsive to young people's interests and concerns. Still, these online components were seen as add-ons to the basic library, which was always the building.

Even the best library website for children pays little attention to the building with which it is connected. The traffic flow is imagined as a one-way process; the website is a portal to the "real" library, which is built of bricks and mortar. Library design awards are given solely for the quality of the building "housing" the library. If the library is defined, however, in terms of its provision of services, as Drotner (2009) suggests, rather than as a collection, the design should be evaluated in terms of all of its service provision points, not just the building. Chapter 8 suggests some ways of creating a blended library that exists with or without a building.

8

———◆·◆———

DESIGNING A BLENDED LIBRARY

Every public building contains a metaphor—a vision of what the building represents. Buildings are designed to reflect their function in physical form. Early children's libraries were thought of as schools, learning spaces for children. Whether consciously or unconsciously, furniture and collections were chosen to conform to this idea of what the library should be. As years passed, and younger children were welcomed into the library, the idea of service shifted to the library as a home-away-from-home, or a playroom. Collections became more varied, offering a wide range of beneficial entertainment and recreational activities. In recent years, various metaphors have been exemplified in library planning and design, including

- library as exploration and adventure,
- library as secure place in a dangerous world,
- library as a child-designed fantasy world
- library as a shopping center for the community, and
- library as a theater: "We imagined the library as a theatre—'the stage' where the users meet the magic of the library and get the chance to interact—'the store of set pieces' to ring the changes and 'the backstage' for the staff" (Lunden 2009).

Each of these different views of a library can serve as inspiration for building a useful library facility, but perhaps it is time for a new metaphor—the blended library. This envisions the library not as a building set in a specific location, but as a web of information and services spreading out to all members of a community or area. Such a library would serve its community at home, in schools, outdoors, and in buildings or rooms that could be scattered geographically.

COMPONENTS OF A BLENDED LIBRARY

Blended libraries may vary in what they offer to the public, but there are several components that are likely to be included:

- Library portal
- Interfaces—variety for various hardware
- Collection of materials—some print, others electronic
- Staff to organize content and link with users
- Communication devices
- Place for face-to-face meetings

In this chapter, we look at each of these components in turn.

LIBRARY PORTALS

A library portal physically can be merely a doorway or any entrance to a library building, but in a symbolic sense, it is not the entrance to a building, but an entrance to the information available in the library. An early 20th-century version of a library portal is shown in the image of the New York Public Library in Figure 8.1.

This design calls attention to the value of the material within the library by the solidity of the structure and the formality of the columns reflecting classic treasures. Variations on the design of a library as a storehouse of collected wisdom were used throughout the 20th century as appropriate portals to libraries.

Figure 8.1   New York Public Library. Photo courtesy of www.airninja.com.

The portal serves as an entry point to the library, but the entrances to the New York Public Library and other libraries of that era do not offer any direct view of resources available inside. This can be a barrier to individuals who are unfamiliar with what a library might contain. The similarity of the outside of public buildings can sometimes be confusing to people unsure of their function. The entrance to the Metropolitan Museum of Art, for example, is very similar to the New York Public Library, with similar wide, shallow steps and Greek columns framing the main doors. Many public buildings provide similar portals, and some librarians consider this a weakness of traditional library architecture. Once a patron enters the library, she is confronted with a choice of which room or department to enter. Often, the books and other materials are not visible from the entrance and can seem to a novice user an almost inaccessible hidden treasure.

As the 20th century entered its second half, library buildings designed to offer a more welcoming entrance began to appear, and by the early 21st century, libraries had taken on a very different look. The Seattle Public Library, built in 2004 (www. spl.org), with its expanse of glass walls, exemplifies the concept of a library as an open institution, offering glimpses of the materials within and the patrons and staff using them. The purpose of the building is clearly visible from the outside, with its view of shelves of books. Adults may quickly become accustomed to finding their way to the particular area they want to visit. For children encountering the library for the first time, however, both the New York Public Library and the Seattle Public Library buildings would be awe-inspiring but perhaps not entirely welcoming.

Secondary Portals—Entrance to the Children's Department

Early public libraries built in the late 19th or early 20th century were designed primarily as quiet places for individuals to read and study. Some libraries did not admit children under 14, and those that did were concerned about the noise and disruption children might cause. Many of the Carnegie libraries, built in the early 20th century, had a children's room on a separate floor from the adult department. When libraries started welcoming young children into the library, most libraries began planning children's departments on the same floor as the adult section. Libraries were often designed with a clearly marked separate children's room, and many libraries today continue that pattern. Some buildings, both new and old, have sharply marked room divisions that cannot be changed without major renovations, which would often be prohibitively expensive. The entrance to the children's department thus becomes a portal to a special area set aside for children and their parents to find books and other materials especially chosen for them.

Other libraries built in the late 20th century, especially small libraries and branches, chose a different and more open design. The entrance to the children's room is marked only by a change in décor. Open-plan libraries offer free movement of patrons from one section of the library to another. The "portal" to the children's department is deliberately minimal, marked only by a change in the size of furniture and the types of material in the collection. The idea behind this type of plan is to encourage older children to move into the teen or adult department when they are ready to use the resources there and to return to the children's department whenever they choose.

Both arrangements—the separate children's room and the open plan—have their supporters. An open plan allows parents and staff to keep an eye on children

Figure 8.2   Entrance to children's department, Redwood City (CA) Public Library.

without being required to remain in the children's room with them, but the separate children's room keeps the noise down in the adults' space and allows more
freedom for programming and activities in the children's room. Either style is acceptable, but librarians should be aware of the implications of their choices.

What Message Does the Portal Send?

In an open-plan library, children are visually part of the wider library. Their activities will be seen by adults, and whatever noise is made in the department may be
heard in other parts of the library. The children, in turn, can watch what adults
are doing in the library. They may hear snippets of conversation or sounds meant
for other adults. They may accidently wander into the adult stacks and look at
materials meant for adults. Whether this is beneficial or limiting, the children are
definitely a part of the wider community.

When a library has a specific room set aside for children, the department becomes much more self-contained and at the same time more isolated. Activities in
the children's room can be less restrained, more active, and noisier because they
are unlikely to interfere with adult activities. Collections are limited to materials
selected as suitable to the age range, and there is no possibility of children wan-
dering into adult materials unless they actually leave the room. Computers in the
children's room can have filtering and can be restricted to use by children more
easily than in an open-plan library. This gives more freedom to children's librarians

to implement a child-friendly atmosphere, but the disadvantage may be that they make the children's room so cozy and appealing that some children are frightened of moving away into the adult department.

Sub-Portals—Access Points within the Library

Although the purpose of the newer libraries is to make materials and services easier to access, there are still several steps to be taken before reaching the specific item or information the patron is seeking. Most materials are stored on long shelves in a non-intuitive order. Classification systems are an excellent way of locating items in a library, but the structure of the system has to be learned. Librarians and frequent library users may memorize the major categories, but novice or infrequent users seldom do. Let's use Figure 8.3 to look at some of the differences between the way information searches are conducted online and in libraries.

A comparison of these two methods using the phrase "fish of the Amazon River" retrieved nothing from the library card catalog search, either using quotation marks or omitting them, but several relevant websites were found on the Google site

	Catalog searching	Computer searching
First step	Connect to library online catalog (sometimes requires entering library card number).	Find Google search blank on webpage.
Deciding query topic	Decide whether to search author, title, subject heading, or keyword.	Step unnecessary.
Entering topic	Click on type of search and type word; for phrase, use quotation marks.	Type in word or phrase.
Possible errors	Capitalization and spelling must be correct, or search will be unsuccessful.	Capitalization is irrelevant. Obvious spelling errors are automatically corrected. Alternative spellings are suggested.
Results of search	Precise item is usually found if it is in the collection. Narrow range of relevant materials fitting the keyword requested. Information returned is reliable based on credibility of library.	A list of many sites is usually returned. The most relevant are supposed to be at the top. Some sites are unreliable or reflect different meanings of the search term (e.g., sharks as fish and Sharks as hockey team).

(*continued*)

	Catalog searching	Computer searching
Locating information required	Catalog lists information with classification number; material must be located on shelf by searching for correct number (e.g., 944.361/H7837s/2002).	Click on link to website listed. Information frequently available on front page; occasionally, several clicks are required.
Possible undesired outcomes	Frequent failure to get any matches, especially when using keyword searches.	Frequent delivery of so many sites that user is unable to choose the most relevant.
	Occasional failure to locate information on shelf after getting the listing.	Frequent listing of unreliable sites with unverified or false information.

Figure 8.3   Comparison of searching methods.
Note: For this example, the Dewey Decimal system is used as the library classification system and Google is used as an example of an online searching tool. This is only to simplify the comparisons. In reality there are several different choices for each of these operations.

without quotation marks. It is small wonder that many library patrons, particularly younger ones, have turned to online searching as their major information provider.

The library catalog can be considered an additional portal that must be navigated to enter a library. For many patrons, it can feel like a barrier keeping the materials difficult to find or even inaccessible, in contrast to the quick results seen in a computer search. When the internet and search engines for locating information on it became available, many patrons decided that entering a physical library was unnecessary. In response, libraries began to offer online portals.

ONLINE PORTALS

A more recent version of a library portal is the website for the Los Angeles Public Library (see Figure 8.4).

The website portal offers immediate access to several different departments in the library, each of which is clearly visible to the patron, unlike physical libraries where a specific department may be accessible only by walking several yards or by climbing stairs or using an elevator. When public, academic, and school libraries began building websites, their purpose was often to serve as publicity for the library buildings. The information provided was a listing of library locations and hours as well as access to the library catalog. All of this was meant to facilitate visits to the library, and the websites served that purpose well.

Today's websites, in contrast, are not as often an enticement to visit the physical library as they are an alternative way of accessing the library collections. When patrons, whether adults or children, want to access library materials, they may choose to go to a building or they may instead decide to visit the website and find electronic materials. The website portal has become just as important an entrance to the library as the physical portal. Using either one of these two entrances should be a seamless experience; their design should echo one another so that the patron who has learned to navigate one will find it easy to switch to the other.

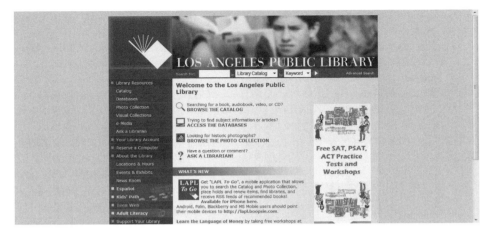

Figure 8.4 Homepage of the Los Angeles Public Library. *Source:* http://wwwlapl.org.

How Can the Blended Library Coordinate Its Designs?

Library buildings are designed to provide a welcoming atmosphere and encourage patrons to use library services. Online portals should be equally carefully planned to provide an inviting welcome. Websites should be designed as complementary portals to the physical building, so that a patron visiting the library homepage will be reminded of the physical library and the connection between the two portals. If possible, navigation of the website should be similar to access in the building. There are a number of steps a children's department can take to coordinate its physical portal with its online portal:

1. As a first step, use similar color scheme for children's website and children's room. A children's department with sunny yellow walls and furniture in shades of green and russet can be visually related to a website that uses the same color scheme. If the entrance to the children's section in the building has a sign saying "Kids' Zone," the website can have a sign with the same heading for the opening page. A child clicking onto the website at home will be quickly reminded of the library room and will be likely to feel at home there immediately.
2. Use the same terms for both online and physical actions—with "search services" rather than "reference services," searching online and searching the catalog can be blended.
3. In the area of responding to resources, online or in-person feedback should be interchangeable. There should be an opportunity for blog or wiki posts and email to library staff.
4. For locating print items, possibly use Google-like maps to pinpoint location. In a one-room library, each catalog entry could be accompanied by a picture of the floor plan with the location of the item (or section) highlighted. As QR codes (short for Quick Response, a form of barcode readable by a machine or mobile phone) become more common in libraries they can be used to pinpoint book locations.

5. The events listing on the webpage can be similar to the listing on a library bulletin board.
6. The website can offer streaming video of library events for children who could not attend in person. Online viewers should not be second-class patrons.
7. The website can include a slideshow of covers of new books. The same slideshow could be shown on a monitor in the library

See Figures 8.5 and 8.6 for an example of how a website can be designed with the specific goal of echoing the look of the children's department library.

In this example, the green sign on the physical entrance to the children's department is carried over to the website design as the heading for the children's page. The large graphic of a giraffe in the children's room becomes the motif for the department's blog, Giraffe Jottings. This marks the website as clearly being an extension of the department and an integrated part of library service.

Another important point is that the homepage of the library itself has a clear link to the children's webpage, making it easy for both children and parents to find. That is demonstrated on the design for a homepage in Figure 8.7.

Note that in this example, the picture of the entrance to the children's department is the Menlo Park Library, but the website examples are purely hypothetical

Figure 8.5 Entrance to children's department, Menlo Park (CA) Public Library.

Figure 8.6 Design for webpage for children's department. Design by d'Wylde Studios.

designs for an imaginary library. The idea of linking a website to the real décor of a physical library could be implemented in any setting.

Online Portals for Mobile Devices

Many adults and an increasing number of young people prefer to access website information from a mobile device rather than a computer. This trend is likely to increase in coming years. There are two ways of handling the problem of making website content available on mobile platforms: keeping the basic website simple enough to be viewed on a small screen or designing a separate website for mobile devices. Designing a separate website is preferable, but this method is also more expensive and requires additional time for updating and maintenance. Librarians should be sure to think through the additional costs, especially in staff time, and plan carefully.

Here are several points to remember in planning a website for mobile access:

- Keep the screen simple and uncluttered.
- Do not repeat navigation on each page.

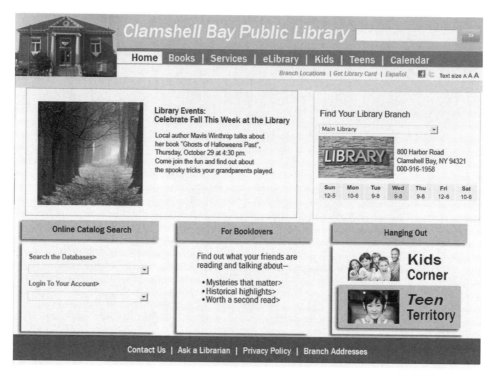

Figure 8.7 Design for homepage of library. Design by d'Wylde Studios.

- Distinguish items from one another by the use of color and different type (mobile devices have small screens and may be difficult to read).
- To avoid mistakes, list a menu of items from which to select rather than asking the user to enter text.
- Do not try to include all the website information on the mobile site—choose only what is essential.

Feedback on mobile interfaces is vital for keeping the site user-friendly. Having a panel of parents, young people, and other mobile users can provide important information about what is working and what is not. Most people enjoy having their opinions asked, and because mobile devices are frequently updated, young people often enjoy testing interfaces and features as they are modified.

The availability and use of mobile devices change quickly over time. Librarians need to keep up with new products and studies of their use. Conferences and library journals are valuable sources of information, as are online user groups, wikis, and websites. If possible, one member of the staff can have specific responsibility for informing the staff about new developments and making suggestions about mobile technology.

BLENDING PHYSICAL AND ELECTRONIC MEDIA

Materials in a blended library include a variety of formats both traditional and new, so librarians will have to decide how to integrate all of the resources available.

Print and Print-Based Materials

Printed books will certainly be a part of the mix, especially for picture book formats and fiction books. Traditional books meet the needs of many children and parents. They are easy to use in the library or at home and do not require any equipment. They can be read to an individual child or to a group or by a single child. This format is unlikely to disappear in the lifetime of today's children.

Enhanced books on a screen, whether projected for a group or handheld by individuals, are also likely to be popular. Picture books with sound effects, musical accompaniments, or spoken dialogue can be offered on electronic devices and this use is likely to increase. Video clips are sometimes inserted into picture books and children's fiction and nonfiction books. The role of a public or school library in supporting and circulating electronic material is likely to vary in different communities.

1. If most families in a community have the device (for example, an iPad or a similar product), libraries might serve as a reviewing and evaluation source for suggesting to parents and children new materials available for downloading.
2. In communities where many families do not have access to the hardware, libraries might buy the devices and lend them out to users. Users could then download materials in the library under a licensing agreement.
3. An alternative economic model might follow the example of Playaways in which an audiobook is mounted in a throwaway cassette box. Some devices might be designed to handle only one story, or perhaps one series, and these could be owned by the library and made available to users.

Visual Electronic Materials

Visual materials for both recreational and research purposes are an important part of children's library collections. The format of visual materials is trending toward digitally stored videos that can be downloaded to computers, mobiles, and other devices for viewing. DVDs are likely to be less usable as a source for visual material because fewer patrons will want to bother with disks when they can stream videos directly to their computers or mobile devices.

Many reference materials for children are available on commercial video storage sites such as YouTube and other sites. The New York Public Library, for example, has a YouTube channel that provides images and audio archives in its collection and also offers information on additional materials at the library. Other public libraries around the world provide some historical images and information on their sites. An example is the Dublin City Library in Dublin, Ireland, which hosts images and text histories of architectural and industrial sites in the city; for example, see this history of Drimnagh Castle: http://www.youtube.com/watch?v=fF9Q6TnHc_4. The Library of Congress also has a range of visual materials available on its website. Using a video to tell the story of women workers during World War II, the Library of Congress provides authentic and accessible information about an important historical period in America: http://www.youtube.com/watch?v=04VNBM1PqR8. The YouTube channel gives libraries access to more memorable historical information than many history textbooks and makes it available both to good readers and to those who struggle with information in printed form.

A children's department or school library could develop its own video channel on YouTube or another site to house archives of its activities and resources. This would be an ideal activity for a youth group in the library. With the cooperation of teachers and schools, and perhaps funding from community businesses, young people could videotape historic sites in their community and recount their history. They could also record special events in the community such as the visit of a notable public official, a county fair, or an ethnic parade. These records are comparatively inexpensive to produce and provide a valuable historical record of a community. They also offer young people valuable training in filming and encourage cohesive community sympathies.

Although video materials are often what children think of when they are looking for images, still pictures are also important. There are many searchable depositories of online images that can be used for research. The Library of Congress has a large collection that can be accessed. Local images can often be stored on the library's own site, although centralized depositories for images may be used for a library district. One of the challenges of giving children access to image archives is to teach them about copyright, so that they understand they should follow the rules for using images in reports or other written work.

Digital materials always require some equipment to make them usable. The trend today is for personal mobile equipment to be owned by many individuals. In some communities, almost every young patron over the age of 10 has a mobile phone or MP3 player that can be used to access audio and visual media. Whether this trend will continue and become almost universal, so that libraries can count on patrons having their own viewing or listening equipment, remains to be seen. As of 2010, most library use of visual materials depends on the availability of computers. Almost all libraries have computers for patron use in the library. Online material recommended by the library can be accessed through computers at home or at school. There are still many young people, the majority in some communities, who do not have access to the internet at home and whose access time in school is limited. As library materials become more digitized, libraries will have to find ways to make the materials available to all potential patrons. This will require budget decisions that balance the cost of materials and the cost of machines to make the materials accessible.

Technology will undoubtedly change over the years, and transitions to updated platforms are an important part of maintaining digital records. This costs money, but maintaining a usable collection always involves some cost. This kind of project may attract funding from community groups, businesses, and foundations. Young people can be trained as volunteers, and cooperation with local schools may make it possible to integrate the activities as part of an educational program.

As the proliferation of communication devices provides a glut of information and recreational materials, the library's role will more and more become that of evaluating and recommending materials rather than necessarily supplying them. This will make the collection more flexible and less permanent than those that libraries provided in the past. Patrons, however, will still want to be able to find favorite materials for repeated use, so collections cannot be throwaways. Semi-permanent storage will be needed for some materials, although public libraries are unlikely to maintain permanent collections of outdated children's materials. Most children's books and other materials have a time-limited appeal. Some classics remain popular for 20 years or more, but the majority cease to interest children after 5 or 10 years. Maintaining a permanent collection of children's books will be the task of research libraries. Public libraries are generally intended to be living collections of frequently used materials. Information in most fields becomes outdated quickly, so informational material should be weeded frequently as knowledge in the field grows and changes. Recreational materials are also replaced by newer versions. Children's libraries have never been much concerned with the preservation of historical materials, and they are likely to be even less so in the future.

Provision for Face-to-Face Interactions

Although access to library information and materials is likely to move off-site in the future, most communities will still want to provide a physical location for administration of the library and for providing some patron services. Many communities have already invested heavily in library buildings, and very few people would want to give these up. For the next half century at least, library buildings will be an important part of service, although the design and size of these buildings may change considerably.

Just as physical schools serve an important purpose, not only in educating children but also in teaching them shared cultural norms and giving them practice in social interactions, so too libraries offer unique experiences that would be difficult to replace online. Infants and toddlers need the physical presence of other human beings to become functioning members of society. Storyhours for very young children provide a range of experiences—seeing, hearing, interacting with adults and peers, and enjoying the security of touching their parent or caregiver. It's unlikely that a community would want to give up this activity.

For school-age children too, face-to-face interactions with their peers provide important social experiences. Most online groups, such as reading clubs, are more successful when the online component is strengthened by periodic meetings. Online interactions are usually more satisfying when they are conducted between people who have also met one another face-to-face. Programming activities in libraries are likely to become a mix of electronic and physical interactions rather than go completely online.

Another factor that may influence the development of libraries is the growing trend toward online education even for elementary school children. Some charter schools now offer online curricula for children starting in the first grade. These schools rely on parents to coordinate the lessons and to monitor their child's activities, so the experience is much like homeschooling, but with an online component. The schools are designed to offer each student a self-paced individualized educational experience. The pace at which students encounter the lessons, the speed with which they cover each topic, and the length and timing of vacation periods are controlled by the parents and the children rather than by the calendar of a school district as with traditional public schools.

Self-paced education using a variety of resources is precisely what public libraries have offered to adults and young people over the years. If online education for elementary and high school students becomes a dominant format, it might open a new area of service for public libraries. Librarians are already trained to evaluate and recommend materials for schoolchildren, so they could offer valuable supplementary materials. They can also offer students whose schooling is being delivered online a safe, congenial location in which to have face-to-face interaction with other children and with trained adults. Just as groups of homeschooling parents often rely on libraries for support material and for an education-focused meeting place, public libraries could offer similar support for students of online schools. This is a natural outgrowth of the work already being done by most public librarians. It is too early to predict how widespread online elementary education will become, but librarians will want to be aware of trends and consider how the library could become part of the process. Even if the majority of children in a community continue to go to traditional public schools, these schools are likely to offer at least some courses online. Public libraries can be natural partners in this work.

Staffing for Blended Libraries

The Competencies document published by the Association for Library Service to Children groups its standards in several categories:

- knowledge of the client group,
- administrative and managerial skills,
- communications skills,
- materials and collection development,
- programming skills,
- advocacy,
- public relations and networking, and
- professionalism and professional development.

These categories cover the basic skills needed by children's librarians, but they are based on a work environment concentrated in a library building. As library buildings decrease in importance, and much library work is done electronically at a distance, the skills will have to be modified. One obvious change is an increasing need for technology skills. If a majority of patrons are using library resources and expertise from outside the library, it will be impossible to hand off all technology issues to a specialized IT staff. Librarians themselves will have to be able to evaluate and choose the equipment they require to keep their collections and services usable. They will also have to have the know-how and confidence to give instruction in using equipment and to troubleshoot minor difficulties with computers and other technology tools. Continuing education in technology skills will be an increasing responsibility for the library and for individual staff members.

More important than the technology skills will be an increasing need for communication skills that can be used on a variety of platforms and through different media. Face-to-face communication will remain important. Many of today's librarians are accustomed to using texting, email, and social media for communicating with their peers. Talking to children online offers different challenges, but it is a skill that can be mastered. The age level of the child determines the tone and content of communication, but even young children are becoming accustomed to asking and responding to questions online, whether through voice or, as they become more fluent, in writing. Librarians who can project a friendly image on many platforms are a great asset to their libraries. In some libraries, even today, patrons at a distance, whether on the phone, email, or texting, do not get as much attention as those who are present in the library. This attitude will change as more library communication becomes electronic.

The most important skill required of children's librarians as libraries go through the immense changes of the next several decades is the ability to absorb new information and examine existing attitudes and guidelines. For many years, libraries have been accustomed to measuring change in years, but it is likely that coming changes will occur on a speedier timetable. (For further discussion of staff training, see chapter 9).

OVERVIEW OF THE BLENDED LIBRARY

The convergence of media in recent years has had a revolutionary effect on libraries. The traditional view of the library as a storehouse of packaged information will change as the internet disperses information throughout the community. Librarians must analyze ways in which young people and their parents will use the library in years to come. Although it is impossible to predict with certainty what the future holds, this chapter has discussed some of the decisions that will have to be made about integrating services and collections. Libraries will have to reconsider some basic components of library service, including the design of library buildings, the provision of online access to libraries, the nature of collections, and the changing demands placed on library staff. A successful transition to the new world of media will ensure the survival of public libraries as a vital part of modern society.

SECTION IV

PREPARING TO MEET THE FUTURE

9

PREPARING FOR SERVICE IN THE NEW CHILDREN'S LIBRARY

Many children's librarians working today began their careers at a time when children's libraries were largely collections of books for children to read and enjoy. The revolution in technology that has changed the way children get their entertainment and information has also changed the skills, knowledge, and responsibilities of librarians. Children's librarians play an ever-greater role in helping children gain access to information and entertainment in all formats.

As mentioned in previous chapters, libraries are shifting the focus of their service from offering only collections of materials to being access points for many forms of entertainment and information. This change in function requires a change in attitudes, knowledge, and training of library staff. For example, in the past, it might have been considered adequate if a staff member helped a child to find a book to read at home. In today's library, and the library of the future, there are likely to be far more options for a child's interaction with a book or other library material. A child who borrows the latest award-winning book may follow up in various ways:

- Posting a comment on the library blog
- Sending a text message to a group of friends about the book
- Preparing a video book review for the library website or podcast
- Entering the library's Facebook site to discuss the book with friends

Children's librarians are expected to be able to help children find, enjoy, and use all of the resources of the library, including traditional materials and services as well as the newest technological possibility. Librarians must act as professional guides and teachers, not just as custodians of books. More than that, the librarian in charge of a children's department must assume responsibility for ensuring that all staff members can offer appropriate support for library services.

The work involved in running a children's department has increased and is likely to increase even more in the future. As a result, children's librarians will have less time to spend on individual one-to-one services with children in the library and will have to accept the task of managing services to be carried out by others. There may be some resistance to this idea on the part of children's librarians who think of their work as an individual service to children. Some children's librarians like to think of themselves as practitioners rather than administrators, but today's children's librarian is primarily a manager. A children's department is a complex operation that requires the same kind of planning and organizational skills as a business operation.

LIBRARIANS AS MANAGERS

Children's librarians in this complex world of media are primarily professional managers. As managers, they must understand the three basic components of the operation—*the children they serve, the materials and services with which to serve them,* and *the methods for building support for their services in the community.* This chapter looks at the how a librarian can handle these components and put the pieces together to organize a coherent plan of service.

The tasks of children's librarians reflect the goals of library service to a specific group in the community. To carry out the tasks effectively, the librarian must be informed in the following areas:

- Understanding the audience
- Knowing the community
- Planning a program of services
- Evaluating services
- Marketing the library

Understanding the Audience

First of all, librarians must understand the children they serve. There are tremendous changes in children during their first 12 or 14 years, so we can divide them into groups.

Preschool Children

Preschool children start as infants brought to the children's department by parents or caregivers. Books of nursery games and rhymes for reading to babies as well as recorded music and simple DVDs serve these youngest clients. Many libraries offer storyhours for infants with their parents or caregivers. Librarians know that language development and emerging literacy are enhanced when babies and young children hear stories, rhymes, and other language from their parents. When children reach the toddler stage—about the age of 18 months, when they begin to walk—the range of materials and services increases. Toddlers require special materials—sturdy board books, music CDs, and appropriate DVDs as well as toys. Encouraging parents to provide these materials for their children is an important part of library work.

By the time children reach the age of three or so, their needs and behavior are quite different from those of toddlers. Children of this age can handle standard picture books, and a wide range of materials should be available to meet their varied and growing interests. They are becoming used to seeing information on a screen, whether in the form of television, computer screens, or mobile electronics (see chapter 2). In many libraries, some computers are designated for use by preschoolers and their caregivers. Because preschoolers are interested in learning about almost everything, they are an appreciative audience for library programs. Many of the programs and services provided by traditional children's departments are aimed at preschool children and their needs. It is often during this period that children with special needs are identified, and librarians try to work with parents and caregivers to provide the materials and services required by these children.

School-Age Children

Children between the ages of 5 and 12 are generally considered to be of school age, whether they are enrolled in a school, homeschooled, or in some special situation. Some of these children have a school library available as well as the public library. Children in private or religious schools and homeschooled children often rely on the public library for materials and programs; and in these times of budget cuts and low support for school libraries, many children in public schools also turn to public libraries for help with their schoolwork. During the summer vacation months, many libraries provide special programs and reading clubs for school-age children.

In most communities, there is heavy use of the library by schoolchildren for both recreational and school-related materials. Many of the materials in an average children's department are suitable for this age group. Most of the reference service provided in the department will be for this age group, so the reference collection is usually slanted toward their needs. Because schoolchildren usually visit the library in the late afternoon, evenings, weekends, and holiday periods, they may strain the resources and services of the public library during these times. Many public libraries provide collections and programs specifically to help children with their homework. More and more jurisdictions have cut back on funding for school libraries, and many elementary schools have no certified teacher librarians, so public librarians often step in to help fill the gap. They may work with local schools and teachers to coordinate library services for students.

Adults

Adult users of a children's department include adults choosing books for children—for example, parents, grandparents, teachers, daycare workers in the community, and students of children's literature. Children's librarians should be prepared to understand the needs of adults in the children's room and provide resources for them.

Knowing the Community

Library services are based on the needs of the community; every community has an individual profile that determines the type of materials and services required. These needs can be studied through learning about the demographics and conducting personal observation.

Demographics

Knowledge of these basic factors is an important base on which to build library services:

- Population size and trends
- Ethnic, racial, and cultural groups represented
- Educational levels
- Age levels
- Income levels

Demographic factors such as ethnic composition and income levels can change quickly in a community, so the librarian needs to be aware of the latest trends. Community planning groups and city governments often collect this kind of information.

Library Statistics

Statistics on registration, circulation, use of the library's online services, and program attendance give additional information about library users in the community. In designing a departmental program, it is useful to break down library statistics by age level. If this is not done routinely, a sampling system can be used to obtain an approximation. Statistics about the materials used by children in the library and accessed through library sources can provide a wealth of information concerning the popularity of particular types of material and services:

- Circulation of graphic novels compared with standard format
- Non-English-language books or other materials used
- Format of audio materials preferred
- Most popular nonfiction subject areas
- Types of reference questions asked
- Circulation of easy readers, picture books, and chapter books

Observation

Armed with background demographic knowledge about the community, a librarian can make direct observations. Reading the neighborhood weekly newspaper and watching local television news gives insight into community interests. A few hours spent walking around the community and visiting local shopping outlets will provide information about the type of housing prevalent in various areas and the range and price levels of goods in stores. The number, ages, and activities of children visible on the streets and in parks and malls provide information about their interests and needs. Systematic observation can be as valuable as formal data for learning more about a community. Also, talking with children, parents, and teachers to find out where children spend their time outside of school, what issues concern the community, and what is new or changing is an important way to keep up with community news.

Planning a Program of Services

A librarian who has gathered the important information about the potential patrons who will be served and the background information about the community is ready to start planning a program of services. Most libraries offer a basic menu of collections and services for children, although the details and methods of delivery vary from one community to another. Each type of service is distinct, but they operate together to create the complete program of service. Such services include the following:

- Building collections
- Making the collection accessible
- Delivering information services
- Providing educational and recreational programs
- Forming partnerships in the community

Building Collections

The key to building attractive and useful collections for children is knowing the materials available, evaluating them, and choosing the ones that are most attractive and suitable for the children in the community. Publishing is a thriving industry, and thousands of new children's books are produced every year; no single librarian can examine each one of them. When in addition to books, a library is committed to providing many other types of media, the task of selecting the best of them may seem overwhelming. For this reason, it is important to have a collection policy for each type of material the library provides, one that makes clear the overall balance of the collection, which sources will be used to locate materials for purchase, and who is responsible for making decisions about purchases. For example, in book selection, the policy would state what proportion of the books should be for preschool children and how many should be for children of school age, how many should be primarily recreational and how many should be primarily information resources. Often, libraries decide they will spend certain percentages of their book funds on fiction and nonfiction, perhaps 60 percent on fiction and 35 percent on nonfiction. Books for reference would take up the other 5 percent, although spending on reference books for children's collections is decreasing. Some libraries use all of the reference money for the children's department on database costs. Establishing goals and determining in advance where the money should be allocated makes it easier to be systematic in building collections, so standards should be set for each type of material purchased.

To establish realistic goals for a collection, the librarian will consider what has been learned about the community and the potential patrons:

- Are most of the children in the area preschoolers, or are more of them in middle or high school?
- Do the children come to the library to find information that will help them in school, or do they most often look for recreational materials?

- Which books are most popular? Circulation figures help librarians understand which of the older books remain popular and what children are looking for in new books.

- Are most children in the community comfortable with using computers and other electronic devices to access information?

- Are there ethnic or racial minority groups whose needs must be considered?

- Are many schoolchildren dependent on the public library because of weaknesses in the school libraries or the prevalence of homeschooling?

When the librarian has decided what kind of collection should be built, she can set up a systematic plan for acquiring materials. This would include reading journals or blogs that review materials, establishing relations with publishers, and designing an ordering system. The preceding example used above is for a print collection, but the same principles hold true for other types of materials such as audiovisual or online resources. Several professional journals review audiovisual materials, and some cover websites and other online materials, but not nearly as many as review books. Professional associations are helpful sources for identifying multimedia resources, and the lists provided by the Association for Library Services to Children (a division of the American Library Association) are indispensible tools for the children's librarians. Some state and local associations also offer helpful lists and information.

Parents, teachers, and the children themselves can offer valuable advice about materials that would add to the collection. Every library should welcome patron suggestions through a suggestion box in the library and on the library website and social media pages, as well as through informal channels of conversation and discussion with community groups. The librarian has the responsibility to review materials and choose those that fit the guidelines for the collection, but collaboration with the community is a helpful way to keep up with materials that are available.

The three basic steps for collecting any type of material are the same:

- collect information about needs of potential users,

- evaluate the materials available, and

- establish a process for obtaining them.

Making the Collection Accessible

Librarians are accustomed to cataloging materials to make them easy to find in the library. Online catalogs are the most important tool librarians have for locating and retrieving specific material. Despite changes in the type of media, the catalog is still important and should be available in several formats from both within and outside the library building. Many patrons prefer to consult a catalog from home or school and then go to the library building to pick up materials. This pattern of use is probably going to grow in importance. An online catalog that can be consulted on a home computer, on a mobile phone, or on another platform from any location is a valuable service for the library to offer. The catalog for children's materials should be easy for parents to use and also for children as they become readers. Enhancements such as pictures of book covers are very helpful. A link to the catalog should be easy to locate on the homepage of the library website and usable on both computers and mobile devices. Earlier chapters have discussed some of the ways young people may want to access information about the collection; librarians should be sure that all staff members in the library, including clerical staff, are familiar with the various ways of accessing library materials. Instruction in the use of the library catalog is an important part of service, and both professional and support staff in the department should be able to offer it to patrons.

Delivering Information Services

Information services, often called reference services, are an important component of library service. Questions may be about recreational reading, such as "How many books about Harry Potter do you have?" Or they may relate to subjects being studied in school, such as "How many planets are there, and what are their names?" Traditional library service has assumed that the person asking the question is in the library, but today, many children would like to ask these questions while they are at home or in school. Modern children's departments offer information services through a variety of media and will probably offer more as technology develops further. Reference interactions may take place in many different ways:

- Face-to-face
- Telephone service
- Questions posted on website
- Email questions directly to library staff
- Online chat offered through website
- Text messages sent on mobile devices
- Questions posted on social network site

Traditional reference service, especially to children, has frequently been based on the idea that the librarian finds the print source, and the child should search for the information. A child asking a question such as "What is the population of Argentina?" would be helped to find the reference book with the answer but then would be expected to find the specific information for herself. This attitude on the part of librarians changed somewhat when telephone reference service became standard. A distinction was often made between a "quick reference" question such as the preceding example, which would be answered directly, and an extended question about a subject for which the patron would be given the source and then expected to search for more information in the library.

Today, many families expect information to be delivered to them electronically at home, or wherever they may be. Print sources are rarely of interest because they do not expect to visit the library. Most children and parents sending a question to a librarian through email or other electronic method expect a factual answer to the question (Question: "Who was the first prime minister of India?" Answer: "Jawaharlal Nehru"). Although neither parents nor children often ask for it, the generally accepted library practice is to give a source for each answer. The source is more often a website or other online source than a printed reference book. When the question requires more information than a librarian is willing to include in an answer ("How did the Pony Express service operate?"), the librarian has no choice but to refer to a source that gives detailed information. The patron generally wants an online source, which can be troubling if the librarian knows that an excellent print source is included in the library collection.

The differences between information services given in the library and those given electronically have led to many discussions, but practices in handling them vary widely from one library to another. The most frequently consulted online encyclopedia for children to use is *Wikipedia*, but some teachers and librarians object to this as a source. Certainly, it is preferable to have more than one source, but this may require considerable searching. Developing a set of guidelines for reference services may be a useful project for a librarian to take on. At the very least, a series of discussions with the staff will help to clarify the issues involved in moving from in-person to electronic information services.

Providing Educational and Recreational Programs

Library programs offer opportunities for children to learn about the collection and services. Some of the most popular programs in children's libraries have been traditional:

- Storyhours
- Summer reading programs
- Reading clubs
- Craft activities related to books
- Visits by authors or illustrators

In many traditional libraries, the same type of program has been offered for many years, and the professional staff often spend a great deal of their time working out new approaches and new themes for programs. There is certainly no need to stop having traditional programs, but in some communities, they attract a small, enthusiastic audience but do not appeal to a large percentage of potential library users. As the variety of media coverage expands, offering the possibility of different kinds of programming, the librarian's task is to decide which programs will be most valuable to the widest range of children and families. The choice of programs should be based on knowledge of the community and the children who live there. Rather than offering the same range of programs year after year, the library should review the choices each year and plan services based on specific needs in the community. The librarian's task is to decide the format of the program, including the times at which it will be offered; the library personnel who will run it; and the marketing plan to let the community know about it. With increasing pressure on a librarian's professional time, few will be able to present individual programs; these can be handled by nonprofessional staff or in some cases by volunteers. The librarian's task is to oversee and manage the selection and organization of programs to ensure that they meet the standards of the library.

As an example, a librarian might decide that a reading club for children ages 8 to 12 might be useful because she has found that this age group does not come to the library as often as the younger children do. She knows that many of these children use computers for their schoolwork, and most of them have internet access at home, so she decides an online reading club would work for them. She chooses to start a club that will meet in the library once a month. In between meetings, children will discuss their reading on a club blog. One of the librarians on the staff will participate in the blog and help children to use it. The purpose of the club is to increase the amount of reading done by this age group and to encourage them to choose books on their own.

After designing the program and working out a plan, the librarian decides how best to let people know about it. An invitation will be posted on the library website, and posters and flyers advertising the new program will be available in the library. Some of the flyers will be sent to schools so teachers can distribute them to children. If the library has a page on a social networking site, such as Facebook, the new club will be announced there. The library staff will invite children who visit the library to join the club and to call or text their friends to let them know about the new program.

Once an activity is started, it is very important to evaluate whether it is meeting its goals. After the club has been operating for a few months, the librarian should check to see how many blog entries are being posted, how many children have attended the monthly meetings, and whether the circulation of books has increased. If the club is successful, the librarian can report the success to her administrators and to people in the community. Perhaps a newspaper would print a story about it, or the local television news could interview some participants.

Through careful planning and management, the librarian can change the library's program of activities from a limited service to dedicated library members into a public offering visible to the entire community. High visibility as an important community service will make it easier for the library to make its case for continuing community support.

Forming Partnerships in the Community

The description of this sample book club program contains an element of forming partnerships in the community. Normal good practice includes maintaining contact with teachers about library services. Schools and public libraries serve many of the same children, and working together strengthens both institutions. A librarian should try to establish good professional relationships with schools in the community, including preschools or nursery groups for very young children, private schools, charter schools, and religious schools as well as the homeschooling community.

A librarian can get ideas about which groups might be good partners by studying the community. If church membership is widespread and active, the library may find that church groups offer a good opportunity for publicizing programs. If a church runs a summer day camp, the library might offer programs tailored to that group. Although the library would not offer specifically religious materials, there are many more general programs that would be appropriate to present to church groups. In a community with many residents whose first language is not English, the library may offer dual-language programs for children or offer talks to parents' groups about their children's reading.

The better integrated the library is with the community, the stronger its support is likely to be. Although the major responsibility for maintaining good community relations rests with the chief librarian and administrative staff, the children's librarian can be an important part of that effort. Children's services are often the most popular services a library provides, so they attract many people who might not be interested in or familiar with library work in general. The professional children's librarian should not remain hidden within the children's department but should be part of the management team working actively with community groups.

EVALUATING SERVICES

Rigorous evaluation is a vital part of maintaining quality of services. The method of evaluation should be decided when a program or service is planned, not after it has been offered. Systematic observation and data collection will let a librarian know whether the materials and services provided by the library are meeting the needs of patrons. Following are some useful ways of evaluating services.

Surveys

Ask children or their parents how satisfied they are with the library's collection and services. This can be done through an online or paper survey or by systematically asking individuals when they are in the library. It is usually a good idea to give users many opportunities for feedback on a day-to-day basis as well as implementing formal surveys every few years or whenever a major change is planned. Surveys and feedback opportunities should be available online as well as in the library building. Response rates on library surveys tend to be low, but if users believe their input will have an impact on services, they are more likely to answer questions. A number of online survey tools are available, but the crucial element is the clarity and importance of the questions. A short, clear survey asking for brief replies is better than a longer instrument that many people will not complete.

Statistics

Circulation statistics are important, and so are the number of individuals using the library, the number of visits to the library's website, and the number of reference questions asked. Statistics should also be gathered about the use of the library's website and the number of times individuals have clicked on the children's page. The more facts a librarian has, the more support is likely to be given. Many statistics are routinely collected, and website analytics are easy to obtain, but none of this material is useful unless the librarian takes the time to examine the findings and discuss them with other staff members. Sometimes it is helpful for a librarian to contact a faculty member at a nearby community college or university and ask for help in analyzing the data provided by library statistics.

Observation

It is a good idea to observe and record the number of children who use the library and the materials they use. Ask staff members to make notes about what they see. They should note which materials and services are most popular and which are not being used as often as expected; which reference questions are asked most often; any questions that the library staff cannot answer; and other information of that type.

Facts collected through all these methods will help a librarian plan future services and shape the collection to meet the needs of users.

MARKETING THE LIBRARY'S SERVICES

No matter how good the collections and services in a library are, they will not be used as often as we hope unless people in the community know about them. Like any good manager, the children's librarian develops a plan for marketing library services.

Designing a Marketing Plan

The library as a whole may have a formal marketing plan and a specific individual or department to coordinate marketing for all departments. In other libraries, the departments may be expected to handle their own marketing. In either case, the children's librarian should take responsibility for ensuring that her department plays a prominent role in the library's marketing efforts. In the media-saturated world of the 21st century, many organizations are sending messages to the public; unless the library has a strong, consistent voice, its programs and services may not be recognized. Fortunately, many of the newer technologies have made marketing less expensive and more effective than it was in the past. With planning and effort, the children's department will be able to reach its audience. A children's librarian who knows her community and her library users can build on this knowledge to plan the best ways to publicize the library's activities. Having a written marketing plan for the children's department will help coordinate promotional activities, keep them on target, and make them more efficient and effective.

Being Visible in the Community

One of the most effective ways to reach people is through word of mouth. Encouraging feedback from library patrons and their families will make them feel friendly toward the library and lead many to tell their friends about services. It is often easy to identify the opinion leaders in a community: the mother or father who is active in storyhour programs and seems to know many of the other parents, a sixth grader who attracts a group of friends around him in the library, even a third grader who enthusiastically tells her teacher about the library books she has read—all of these individuals are communicating with their groups and building goodwill toward the library. A good basic step in marketing is to identify specific groups of people who can be counted on to support library programs:

- Parents in preschool programs who can form a library support group
- School-age children who join a group of peer reviewers for new materials
- Teachers who are willing to sign up for a library newsletter or blog
- Representatives of ethnic or community groups who would like to give input about library services

Once these groups are identified, they can easily be kept informed about library programs or new materials and asked for suggestions about services. A monthly email of updates about the library or a special section of the website for library advisory groups will encourage frequent feedback and ideas. Once these individuals are informed and feel themselves a part of the library, they are likely to tell other people about what the library has to offer.

News Releases

A fundamental part of marketing is to send news releases to media outlets about the valuable collections and important services the library is offering. Whenever the library has a visit from an author, illustrator, or storyteller, the library should prepare a short press release and send it to local media outlets. The library's partners—schools and community groups—should be notified about the new books coming into the library and the programs presented. News releases are usually sent by email, so preparing and distributing them is not a very time-consuming task, but it is a very important part of basic marketing.

Using Technology

Marketing has been made easier in recent years by the technology now available. One basic means of letting the public know what the children's library is doing is by having an attractive and informative website. The website can provide most of the important information for patrons:

- Library catalog
- Announcements about activities and new materials
- Library blog for staff and patrons to review new materials
- Links to library groups such as reading clubs
- Links to outside educational websites
- Links to Twitter or other social networking sites for the library
- Practical information about hours and location of libraries

The library website is almost universally used to publicize library collections and services, but many other technology tools mentioned in previous chapters, such as Facebook, Twitter, other social media sites, and blogging, are an important segment of marketing. Chapter 10 gives more suggestions about reaching out to the community, and several books and websites on marketing, which give more specific information about developing effective strategies, are included on the resources pages at the end of this book.

MAINTAINING PROFESSIONAL CONTACTS

In day-to-day work, most librarians associate with the same small group of people, but to grow as a professional, it is important to exchange ideas with other librarians who work in different places. One of the easiest ways to do this is to become an active member of a professional association and to attend professional conferences.

Attending Conferences

Attending a professional conference is expensive in time and money, yet many librarians find them worth the cost. Most public libraries pay at least some of the cost of conferences, especially for librarians who are active in the professional association. Some large professional organizations offer grants to young librarians to make it possible for them to be at conferences. Following are some of the benefits of attending a conference:

- Participating in professional workshops
- Learning from well-known speakers
- Meeting professionals from other libraries
- Examining new materials and equipment at exhibits
- Practicing skills in chairing committees and speaking in public
- Making new friends who share professional interests

Working on Committees

Contacts made at conferences can help librarians solve professional problems, gather new information, and enlarge their view of the profession. The most long-lasting contacts are usually made through committee work. Committees do the day-by-day work of professional associations. They draw up the guidelines for professional standards, discuss criteria for evaluating books and other materials, give awards, and develop publicity tools that can be used in libraries. Professional committees often have the opportunity to see and try out new advances in library technology and practices. They introduce librarians to people in allied fields such as publishing and government.

Keeping in Touch

Libraries support associations because they increase knowledge about the profession and heighten commitment to it. Keeping in touch with your association is made easier by using the electronic mailing lists, blogs, social media, and other tools maintained by associations. It is usually best to set aside a certain period of time, perhaps half an hour in the morning, to keep up with committee work and maintain professional contacts. A good professional association lifts an individual out of a particular job and offers a glimpse of the wider world of librarianship.

OVERVIEW OF A CHANGING PROFESSION

As can be seen from this chapter's discussion, the work of a children's librarian has changed considerably in the past 10 years and is likely to change even more in coming decades. Library education for children's services professionals in the past has often focused on evaluation of materials, primarily books, and the ways to present books to children. Although much of the work of a children's department will still be aimed at choosing materials and encouraging a variety of literacies, the primary focus of a librarian's work will be on management of resources and services rather than on the evaluation of specific items. The tasks of a children's librarian include the following:

- Gathering information
- Planning services
- Evaluation
- Marketing
- Working with others

Library school curriculum and continuing education programs are shifting to incorporate more courses on managing the complex work of integrating many different formats of materials and enabling children to find their way through the maze of informational and recreational materials available. Librarians who are already working in the field will have to continuously update their information and skills to operate effectively in the new environment.

10

———◆◆◆———

MAKING CHANGE HAPPEN

Change is always easier to talk about than to implement, but change in a person or an institution is inevitable and desirable. As Harold Wilson, a former British prime minister, wrote, "He who rejects change is the architect of decay. The only human institution which rejects progress is the cemetery" (BrainyQuote 2010). If libraries are going to continue being an important community resource, they must serve people in ways that are comfortable and helpful to them rather than convenient for the library.

TAKING STOCK OF WHAT YOU HAVE

The first step in making changes is to understand and evaluate what you already have. Assess the strengths and limitations of the department in these areas:

- Space—Is floor space large enough for an increased collection and additional seating? Is the layout of the room usable and the décor modern and appealing?
- Facilities—Are there enough chairs, tables, computers, electrical outlets, internet access? Is the lighting appropriate?
- Collections—Is the print collection well-balanced and adequate for the present and potential users? Are the digital and nonprint collections appropriate and adequate?
- Services—Are reference services being used frequently? Do patrons ask for help, or do they tend to search on their own?
- Staff—Is staff size adequate? Does the staff reflect the ethnic composition of the community? Are most of the staff open to the idea of change and improvement?

No library department is going to be outstanding or even adequate in all aspects of service, but it is useful to consider the areas of your greatest strengths and weaknesses. Understanding your current position helps you to set realistic goals for improving your service to the community.

FINDING ALLIES FOR CHANGE

Colleagues

If several people in the department see a need for change and are willing to work to make this happen, they are the key people to work with. If the department is small, this nucleus may include only one or two people. It would be helpful to find other colleagues in adult services who agree about the need for change and may be supportive in bringing it about. You can't expect unconditional agreement from all of the colleagues who may be interested in working with you. As has been noted throughout this book, this is an age of interactivity, and colleagues expect to have some input into your plans. It is important not to think of yourself as a lonely voice leading a battle to change and update your library department. Invite your colleagues to help, listen to their opinions, respect their points of view, and be willing to modify your own ideas if that will bring along others. No one has a monopoly on good ideas, so listen, learn, and welcome input from others.

Professional Contacts

Colleagues outside of your own library, particularly those in the same community or region, can be very helpful in trying to negotiate change. Many of these people have gone through the same process that you are entering, and so they understand some of what needs to be done. You probably don't see them every day, but it is easy to stay in touch through email, texting, or whatever method works for both of you. Try to arrange face-to-face meetings when you have the opportunity—at conferences or regional events—and keep them informed about what is being planned. And link into networks to which they are connected. Social and business networks such as LinkedIn and Facebook, as well as professional email lists, can keep you connected to others who are working in your field and have the same professional concerns.

Community Members

The patrons of public library children's departments do not have much direct power to make change in the community, but they have a great deal of influence in their families and among their acquaintances. Teenagers, in particular, can be great allies in persuading library and community administrators about the need for changes in library services and facilities. Parents of younger children are also important change agents and can greatly influence public opinion and community leaders. Interactive library services that make children and teens feel important and a part of the library also make them inclined to support library initiatives more than many of the traditional services do. Some traditional services as they have been presented in the past give people the feeling that the library is a rules-based institution set on its own course and unwelcoming of new ideas. The truth is just the opposite—during the last 20 years, libraries have been among the most innovative of all public institutions. Every librarian working today ought to be part of a massive public relations effort to demonstrate to people in the community how well they can be served by public libraries.

If you, as a librarian, are in the process of trying to get your department to move ahead on developing more interactive innovative services, you have natural allies in young people. As a group, they are among the most receptive to new ideas, and many would be thrilled to be invited to be part of a group planning process. Experience in other countries has shown that both libraries and children benefit when they are involved in planning. "Children's participation gives children role rehearsal experiences, uses their intense developmental need for social experiences with peers, offers opportunities to employ their fledgling hypothetical thinking abilities, and channels their enormous emotional and physical energies" (Onal 2009, p. 2) Most children will become enthusiastic supporters of change if they are encouraged to express their ideas and are given the tools with which to express them. One of the side effects of getting ideas from children is that it usually builds a strong bond between the child and the library because each individual feels a part of the enterprise.

STARTING CHANGE

Once you have identified potential allies in making changes, you have to identify the changes to be made. Suppose you are a new manager in a children's department that has a good, solid collection; adequate space and facilities; and a core of dedicated users who fill the slots in the traditional programs being offered regularly. The circulation figures are steady, although use of reference resources has dropped considerably in recent years, and children and their parents seldom ask the librarians for help. The staff has also noticed that children, especially boys, tend to cut back on library use as they reach grades 5 and 6. Also, the attendees at programs are quite representative of long-term residents in the community, but there is a noticeable shortage of some of the newer ethnic groups who are moving into the neighborhood.

You would like to move the department into a more interactive way of working with the community, and when you talk with the chief administrator, she indicates support for that idea. She also mentions the continuing budget pressure the library is under and warns against proposing large expenditures. You look around the department and wonder where to begin.

Start with the Easy Steps

You begin to talk about change with the two other children's librarians and the clerk who handles circulation and storyhour registration. One of the librarians is an active and dedicated storyhour presenter. She has devised a series of seasonal stories that are popular with parents and young children year after year. She says she's willing to see changes but doesn't want to give up her traditional programs. The other children's librarian works part-time and has devoted years to building up a solid core of books and audiovisual materials for the library. She is quite willing to accept changes as long as they don't include having to work with a computer any more than she already does. The clerk has lived in the neighborhood for many years and enjoys interacting with friends and acquaintances among the parents who come to the library. She has organized an elaborate system of registration for library cards and programs, takes care of all the storyhour props, and is fearful of any innovations that might change her routine or jeopardize her job.

Where is the best place to start? One trait that is almost universal among people who work in children's libraries is that they are devoted to children and to children's books. It's a good idea to start with what you all have in common—a commitment to share the treasures of the library with the community. You want to acknowledge that the staff has been working hard and satisfying many patrons with the collections and services now being offered. One of the most important things for a new manager to remember is *to not disown or devalue what has been done in the past*. If you start by saying (or thinking), "We aren't doing a very good job, and we have to change," you are suggesting that what has been done in the past was a failure. Instead, you want to begin by emphasizing that you want to build on all the valuable work now being done in the library. And you want to make clear that you view all your colleagues and staff as allies who are working to do the best possible job for children in the community.

In choosing the project to start with, you need to take account of the budget constraints and also the attitudes of your staff. If the budget is very tight, there is no point in suggesting expensive innovations such as buying all new furniture, changing the room's décor, or adding substantially to the collection or facilities. It is wiser to start making inexpensive changes that can demonstrate your ability to innovate and to have an impact on the library operations. Usually, the least expensive changes can be made in services rather than materials, so that is probably the best place to start.

For your first steps into bringing modern technology into the children's department, you want to look at how it could enhance your already successful programs. Change for the sake of change doesn't serve anyone well; your proposed changes should improve the experience of patrons and, if possible, also make the staff and the library more effective and efficient. An example would be changing a program of storyhours to draw in more participants and attract people from all groups in the community. Your plan might look something like this:

Sample Plan for Updating Procedures for Storyhour Programs

Current status: Storyhours for preschoolers are held weekly on Thursdays at 10:30 A.M. They are grouped in six-week sessions, and parents are expected to register their children. Announcements about the start of each session and the registration procedures are posted on the library website's children's page and on flyers in the library. Bookmark reminders are also placed in children's books as they are circulated for a month before each session starts. The storyhour groups usually fill up with 25 registered attendees. Many participants register and reregister for several sessions. Evaluations from brief surveys given out at the last program in the session are very positive.

Problems: The program overall is seen as a great success, so no major changes are necessary. The only issue is that participants appear to represent only a particular segment of the community. Although there are many recent immigrants in the neighborhood, none of the registrants are from this group. Also, almost all of the parents in the group are stay-at-home parents, even though many of the shift workers at a nearby factory might find the timing convenient for them.

Possible remedies: Statistics on visits to the children's page on the library website show that only a small percentage of people in the community use the page. How could you reach a wider audience, especially among non-users of the library? Some possibilities:

- Notices sent out to mobile phone lists
- Notices in newsletters (management or union) at local factories and businesses
- Email blasts to local church and community group newsletters
- Announcements on Facebook and reminders on Twitter
- All announcements in appropriate languages for babysitters and caregivers
- Videos of some sections of a program posted on YouTube (avoid showing copyrighted images)

Overcoming staff doubts: Tasks that might seem simple to you can be daunting to individuals not accustomed to them. The gap between digital natives and workers of an older generation can cause problems in any job setting. The key to getting full cooperation for new programs or methods is to make it easy for "newbies" to learn how to use new devices. Clear, written instructions on how to send out mass messages or email blasts are helpful. Even more helpful is having a patient individual work with a staff member to make the process easier and more comfortable. Sometimes, a teenage patron or a library page can fill this role. Perhaps one of the parents who attends storyhours frequently or a member of Friends of the Library will volunteer to work with staff on new methods. An important aspect of training staff members is not to make them feel stupid because they are not comfortable with technology that others adopt easily. Hurt feelings can cause lasting damage. Maya Angelou once said, "People will forget what you said, forget what you did, but not forget how you made them feel" (BrainyQuote 2010).

Doubts about the financial impact of changes should be met with a clear picture of the expense involved and plans to persuade your administrator that any additional costs are worthwhile. There is also an environmental argument to be made because relying on electronic transfers rather than paper puts less strain on natural resources. Just be sure to have a succinct pitch for your plan (in management books, often called an "elevator pitch") so you can quickly explain to the library board, media representatives, and members of the public what your plan is and why it is beneficial to the library.

Maintaining Momentum

Once you have introduced a new program or made substantial changes in a traditional one, you want to maintain the momentum and not slip back into an acceptance of the new model as the way things will always remain. It is better to build on the model of change, and there are several ways of doing this.

Evaluating Changes

Evaluation is the key to building support for maintaining and increasing your efforts. The easiest way to find out whether your attempt to build an audience for the storyhour programs is working or not is to collect statistics about first-time registrations. If you have explained the goals of your project, people will know it is not just the number of parents and caregivers attending programs that is the measure, but the expansion of the population that is being served. Following are some of the markers for success in a storyhour program:

- Increase in first-time registrations
- Low rate of dropouts from the program
- Spontaneous positive feedback from the audience
- Increase in circulation of books used in programs
- Increase in traffic to library webpage and Facebook page

More formal evaluation may be useful, especially if your library administration likes documentation. This could be done by written surveys distributed at each program, by a phone survey of registered attendees, or perhaps by taped interviews in the library after a program. Pictures of the group are helpful too and can be used for the library newsletter and website or given to the media. Be sure to get written permission from a parent or guardian for any photographs of children.

Input from the Target Audience

Reactions and suggestions from parents and caregivers are important. If you have attracted a new group of users to the library, you may be able to turn them into committed library fans by encouraging them to become ongoing participants in library planning. Parent advisory groups might be one way to give parents and caregivers a feeling of ownership in library programs. You have to expect that this will take more time than simply making plans with your colleagues; democratic processes are always time-consuming, but they build strong bonds with participants. Parent groups should have clear guidelines for their responsibilities. They should not expect to make major decisions for all aspects of library policy—that is the prerogative of the legally recognized library board or other governing agency. A parent group for the children's department will deal only with programs designed for children, and their role should be to suggest, not to overrule librarians. This point is especially important when it comes to selecting books or removing them from the collection. The department should have a clear selection policy, so that any complaints about materials can be handled appropriately. If an individual wants a book or other material removed, a formal complaint must be made and proper procedures followed to determine what the library will do. The policy should also state that any citizen can suggest books for the collection or give a gift of books or other materials, but the library will determine whether to add the items to the collection.

Parent groups may meet at the library at regular intervals, or they may communicate electronically through an email list or social media platform. To be effective, the group should be limited to parents or caregivers who have a child eligible for the library programs. This type of group is designed to be a working group focused on a particular subset of library activities. General suggestions for the library can be handled through suggestion boxes or any other method made available to the public. An advisory group may work better if it is asked to give feedback on suggestions for specific materials or programs:

- Would you like the storyhour to include videos?
- Would you be interested in bilingual programs? Do you have any suggestions for people who might be able to give such a program?
- When would you prefer storyhours to be held—mornings, afternoons, evenings, or weekends?
- Do you know anyone with musical skills who might participate in a musical storyhour?
- Should the library serve a snack at storyhour programs?
- What themes would you like to see used for storyhours?

Parent advisory groups usually do not attract a majority of the parents who bring children to storyhour; many people are too busy to devote extra time to library programs. These groups can, however, develop a corps of highly motivated individuals who will be strong supporters of library programs.

In designing programs for older children, librarians can encourage the children themselves to become part of an advisory group. Usually, these take the form of teen advisory groups, but somewhat younger tween-age children might also be interested. Again, the guidelines should indicate clearly that the group is advisory on specific issues and plans centered around programs and collections for their age group. These groups are often helpful in making suggestions for programs to attract their peers. The librarian can encourage participation by all groups in the community and try to avoid the formation of a clique of friends who think they are entitled to make decisions for everyone.

As your work continues, you will find other individuals and groups who appreciate what the library is doing and will support your efforts. Teachers in the local schools as well as preschool teachers and homeschooling families often are dedicated library users and can offer input about the services that would help them. Most teachers are very busy and have little time for interaction, but if you can make communication easy for them, they may be willing to send suggestions and ideas for the library.

Discovering What Other Libraries Are Doing

While you are making changes in your own library or branch, others are doing the same in their locations. Networks can generate more ideas than a single individual. Share your experiences and attempts with colleagues, and listen to their accounts of what is going on in their departments. Regional, state, and national library conferences often have several sessions devoted to innovative programs. Not only is it useful to attend the programs, but you also may meet others who share your interests. Having a network of colleagues to support you and offer suggestions is very helpful.

When you discuss or give presentations about programs in your library, try to be upbeat but not give the false impression that everything you do works out well. Admitting weaknesses or even failures in an attempted change may not be easy, but it is the only way progress is made in a profession. Others may have tried to do the same things that you did and learned something about how they can be made to work. Their experience could be very helpful. No change is without consequences, both good and bad, and discussing what has happened should be a normal part of professional discourse. You don't have to dwell on failures or difficulties, but talk about them as challenges that can and will be met.

Conferences aren't the only way to share information. Reading professional journals, blogs, and wikis also serves to keep you in touch with what is going on in the library world.

MAINTAINING CONDITIONS FOR CONTINUAL CHANGE

Change is an ongoing process, not a one-time event. Just as a library's collection is a constant flow of materials coming in and others being discarded, so too the library's service programs should never be static, but should be changed and modified over the months or years. Maintaining a climate for change means setting up good communications systems with your audience. Fortunately, modern tools make this possible and relatively easy.

Setting Up Communications for Marketing

Blogs. Blogs are one of the easiest and most popular tools for communicating with patrons because they are free and do not require much time to maintain. Most libraries use blogs to provide news about programs, services, and new materials added to the library. They are designed to give news rather than to start a conversation. This setup is fine if the purpose of the blog is mainly to inform the public, but a blog that allows comments may build up a stronger audience connection to the library and particularly to the children's department.

Many people who start a blog are disappointed that it doesn't immediately become popular and sought-out. The ease with which we can get statistics on how many visitors the blog has (through Google Analytics and similar programs) can bring disappointment to the new blogger. It is important to remember that the internet is full of information, and millions of blogs and other postings are added every day. Try to be realistic about the number of hits your blog will get; most library blogs have a small but devoted following. Fortunately, a library department has a limited audience to attract, primarily people in the community who have children. Experts in marketing have suggested several strategies for promoting a blog:

- Add the blog link to your email signature and ask your staff to do the same.
- Add the link to your business card and those of staff members.
- Create links on different pages throughout the website.
- Cross-market with your social media site. (Dowd, Evangeliste, and Silberman 2010)

Your blog is likely to get more attention if it includes pictures of library events and short videos. Just about every parent and grandparent will go to a site that contains a picture of one of their children. If the content is interesting and lively, they may continue to check it frequently.

Who is going to write the blog? Ideally, the staff should share the task. If you are the individual originating the idea, you will probably have to post most of the messages until the blog gets established, but you should try to move to shared responsibility as quickly as possible. Individuals may take specific themes—with one person posting on new books and other materials and another posting on events and programs, or one person could specialize in preschoolers and another on older children. You should try to have a new posting at least twice a week; otherwise, the page will grow stale, and you'll lose your audience.

Short postings are more attractive to most readers than longer ones. Try to keep everything short and lively. Post links to a website for those who want longer materials. Or you can break a topic up into two or more postings with a brief "More about this tomorrow." Blogging should not be onerous, but it needs to be consistent.

Allowing comments adds to audience participation, but it takes time to monitor incoming comments. There are many spammers who will post commercial messages with no relevance to the blog at all, and these should be weeded out. It is usually best not to allow anonymous posts and to go quickly through the comments submitted to weed out anything that is obviously inappropriate.

Presence on Facebook. Many libraries have a page on Facebook or another social network, and because most teens and many adults also use Facebook, this is a good place to post events at the library. Facebook is a constant stream of never-ending comments and news, so some librarians are afraid their postings will not be seen because they will be swept away by newer postings. This can't be helped. We have to accept tools for what they can do, and as long as Facebook and similar sites are being followed by patrons, they are worth a librarian's time. They are especially useful to gather registrations for programs. You can post an invitation and get some feedback about how many people will attend. The figure is never very accurate because only patrons with Facebook accounts who have signed up to be friends of the library will get the notice, but at least you will gather those names. The rate of return on Facebook invites is low, but it is a start in the registration process. Look at the Facebook sections in chapter 7 for some tips for posting on social media sites.

Social networks are especially useful for posting pictures of library events. Among the routine follow-up tasks on the day after a special event should be selecting the best pictures available and posting them on the library website and on your social networking account. You also may want to encourage patrons to post their event pictures on their own pages and link to the library's page. Asking for comments and feedback on the event is also helpful in shaping future events.

Twitter. One new tool for interacting with patrons and potential patrons is Twitter.com, a social networking and microblogging site, which allows any registered user to post short messages (140 characters or less) at any time. Like other social media sites, it allows people to follow other people or groups to receive notification very quickly when something is posted. Many reporters, politicians, and media people use Twitter to let their followers know what is happening and what they are doing. Libraries post tweets to remind people of events or services:

Celebrate this Friday the 13th with an Alfred Hitchcock film @ your library.

How did folks cool down before AC? This week in Local History at KC Library.

It's easy to link to a website in a tweet or to a video or audio file, so each message can make it easy for the viewer to return to the library and keep the connection.

When you set up a Twitter account for your library, choose a distinctive image for your profile so your tweets will stand out. It's a good idea to use the library logo and to echo the colors in your website so people quickly identify the source of the tweet.

To keep your Twitter account closely integrated with the rest of your online communications, you want to have a Twitter link on your website and on your blog. People who use Twitter (and quite a few teens do) can sign up to follow your tweets. You can also activate a Twitter account on your Facebook page so your tweets will appear there too. When you get everything set up, you will have a linked system of marketing to get your news and comments out to your patrons from several different media:

- Website
- Blog
- Twitter
- Facebook

When you want to remind your teen advisory council about a meeting, or alert parents to a special storyhour program, you can post a quick tweet and be sure it will be posted on all four sites. People can use the channel they like best. For private messages, of course, you will still use email, but there is some advantage to mentioning meetings and events publicly where even people not included can see them. This keeps the public aware that the library is busy and has many activities for different groups in the community.

One of the advantages of using tweets is that people who are following the library's account can reply to tweets or comment on them. This may add to the information you post; for example, a parent might comment on a posting about a program by tweeting, "I heard this performer last year, and he was awesome," which allows the parent to feel more involved in the program and gives additional credibility to your announcement.

EXAMPLES OF YOUTH LIBRARY MARKETING

Librarians frequently work with innovation and changes. Hearing directly from some of your fellow professionals who have successfully introduced new programs and services can give you a glimpse of how it works.

HEARING FROM TEENAGERS IN SAN FRANCISCO

Jennifer Collins, the teen services specialist at the San Francisco Public Library, has managed the library's teen advisory council for 10 years. The program started as a program in the central library for 12 to 15 representatives of teens from all over the city. Distance and a lack of easy transportation made it difficult for many appointed members to attend the meetings, so Jennifer changed the format and made the advisory council a regional program. There are 9 librarians in the city who work with teens, and these individuals helped to set up advisory councils in several areas of the city, including the Bayview, Chinatown, Sunset, and other branches in various areas of the city. Occasionally, all of the groups get together for a meeting, but for the most part, they work locally on different projects, which the teens choose themselves. The Chinatown branch group, for example, carried out a website design project; Bayview decided to concentrate on presenting programs to other teens, so they changed their name to Speak Up; Sunset chooses different activities, such as scavenger hunts and collecting money for people suffering from disasters such as Hurricane Katrina.

One of the issues that challenge the San Francisco program is the urban environment in which it operates. There has been some parental concern about the safety of teens going to evening meetings in libraries, and urban teens tend to lead busy lives that keep them from devoting much time to the councils. Jennifer wonders if teen councils in smaller communities or suburban neighborhoods are more easily managed than their urban counterparts.

Most council members are suggested by branch librarians, usually from the groups of tween volunteers who work summers on the summer reading programs. Sometimes they are recommended by school librarians or English teachers. There is a notice on the website, and teens occasionally call and ask to join. A recruitment policy has never been set because there has been no trouble in getting enough people to join. Most members are highly motivated, and some get community service credit from their schools. When the program first started, a small stipend was paid to the members, but the students asked that the payment be dropped. They felt that some people were not interested in the work and were coming only because of the payment. Dropping the stipend did not affect the number of recruits or interest in the program. Recognition for members of the group comes in the form of an appreciation party twice a year and a small graduation gift if a volunteer graduates while a member. The teens also are sometimes asked to speak at a Library Commission meeting, which brings some community recognition.

The teen advisory council advises on materials for purchase and the direction and implementation of programs. Members have been asked for suggestions for getting publicity for programs, but they have been fairly traditional in their approaches. They tend not to be technology-oriented except for using Facebook and do not feel the need to communicate electronically between meetings. The groups need a lot of prompting from the moderator, who has to elicit responses. Usually, they are better at choosing between suggested programs than coming up with new ideas. The major problem with the group has been trying to find a focus that keeps them interested. Jennifer has drawn up a yearly calendar with suggestions of things that can be done. Disciplinary problems have been very few and very mild. There are no specific age limits for the group, but members must be in high school. Most are at the younger edge of high school—they are active in their sophomore and junior years, but then most drop out or lower their participation in senior year. More girls than boys join the group, although boys are encouraged.

Jennifer would like to have more focused projects—writing a newsletter or creating a website. The groups did have input about the design of a recently launched new website for the library. They also visited the branches slated for renovation and made suggestions about how to use the space and about the décor. They have also gone to various branches and asked reference questions to evaluate the service.

Jennifer's advice to people starting a teen advisory group is to have a few projects in mind at the beginning and to approach the teens with suggestions that have a definite   outcome. She has found Diane Tuccili's book Library Teen Advisory Groups (2005) the most useful professional resource for her purposes.

BLOGGING FOR PARENTS AND YOUNGER
CHILDREN IN NEW JERSEY

At the Cherry Hill Public Library in New Jersey, a children's department blog called The Wild Rumpus has attracted attention. Meghan MacLauchlan, the library's youth services supervisor for children, described her hopes and plans in starting it:

> I wanted to start a blog for our Children's Department when I started here at the Cherry Hill Library in August of 2007, but never found the time. I thought a blog would be a great way to get "extra" info out to our patrons. We are not able to easily edit our website, but a blog grants us a lot of flexibility. We can quickly post about a book that's being made into a movie, pictures from a great event, a timely book list, or reviews of what we're reading. Our blog is more informal than the library's website, and it allows the Children's Department to come across as a fun and dynamic place.
>
> We were able to bring on more staff in 2009, and at that point I was able to assign one of our new librarians, Alia Shields, the task of getting our blog up and running. We did a lot of surfing the net to see what other libraries were doing and just went for it. We try to post at least once a week, sometimes more frequently. Our main target is parents, and we hope they share posts with their children as appropriate.
>
> The title of our blog comes from *Where the Wild Things Are*. We did not hire a web designer or use a web-master. Alia Shields created the blog using Blogger and a free template that is created at the bottom of our blog page. She edited the template slightly—adding some color and more stars to the header. There are a variety of blog hosting services to choose from. We went with Blogger because Alia had previous experience with the software, and it is more user-friendly. If many staff members will be contributing posts to a blog, ease of use should definitely be taken into consideration. With collaboration in mind, we set our Blogger display name to "Your Children's Librarian." We moderate comments so that we can catch any inappropriate language (so far no issues with this) or spam before it makes its way onto the blog.
>
> At the beginning, it was tough getting readers, but we kept writing into that void! We continued to promote as we could and talk up the

blog during programs, and over the last few months our page views have skyrocketed. We have not tried to publicize in local media, but have publicized in house—linking from our webpage and creating bookmarks and fliers. We make sure to hand out bookmarks at any event where we are taking pictures that will end up on the blog. What parent doesn't want to check out cute pictures of their children?

We are careful about the pictures we post. We get written photo releases and edit the photos to blur nametags. When photo releases are a hassle (at big events), we try to stick with face-less photos—shots from the back of the room or close shots of busy hands and pictures of regulars who we know have photo releases on file. We keep photo releases for a year.

As for future plans, I want to do more with our current blog. I would like to get kids more involved in creating content—perhaps reviewing Advance Reading Copies of books or creating short videos. The blog has been a great success, and we want to build on that to reach even more parents and children. You can take a look at the blog at http://www.chplyouthservices.blogspot.com/.

Figure 10.1   The Wild Rumpus Blog, Cherry Hill (NJ) Public Library. *Source:* http://www.chplyouthservices.blogspot.com.

Keeping Colleagues on Board

While communicating with your patron group, you don't want to neglect colleagues in the library. Everyone who works in the children's department should feel a part of the services. Encouraging staff members to take turns writing blog posts, adding comments to Facebook, or sending announcements out on Twitter will help to build group cohesion. Staff members usually belong to other groups outside the library, and the more enthusiastic they are about what the department is doing, the more likely they are to tell their friends and neighbors about it. They can be the best salespeople for your department and build up a lot of goodwill in the community.

Library employees who work in different departments will appreciate being informed about what the children's department is doing. Posting information on the staff wiki or newsletter and speaking to people informally in the staff room usually builds support for your program, although you have to be careful not to overwhelm everyone with more information than they want. Other departments are also engaged in various projects and events, so you should be prepared to listen as well as talk.

CHILDREN AND CHANGE

Children are natural explorers and agents of change; whether it is Alice bravely venturing down the rabbit hole to face a bewildering new landscape or Curious George testing the limits of balloon power, they face the future with keen eyes and bright curiosity. For more than100 years, librarians and children have been allies in opening doors and finding new worlds.

Librarians welcomed new immigrants into libraries and offered them the best of their heritage literature while encouraging them to sample the books of their new country. When films arrived and later television, children's librarians were among the first to integrate the new formats into their services. Now libraries are facing an even wider change in media use as the internet and its ever-expanding platforms spread not only into libraries, schools, and other institutions but also into almost every home in the developed world. Children's librarians are ready to meet the challenge.

Without giving up the values that have inspired the profession since its beginnings, librarians can adjust services and materials to meet children where they are. They can become a part of the blend of words and images, ideas and technology that will allow all of us to learn to live with the possibilities and limitations of the future that our children will inhabit.

REFERENCES AND FURTHER READING

Abel, David. "Welcome to the Library. Say Goodbye to the Books. Cushing Academy Embraces a Digital Future." *Boston Globe*, Sept. 4, 2009, Metro Section.

American Academy of Pediatrics. Committee on Public Education. "Media Education." *Pediatrics* 104.2 (1999): 342–43.

Anderson, Terry. *Theory and Practice of Online Learning*. Edmonton: AU Press, 2008.

Andronikidis, Andreas I, and Lambrianidou, Maria. "Children's Understanding of Television Advertising: A Grounded Theory Approach." *Psychology & Marketing* 27.4 (2010): 299–322.

Bergman, Ingmar. *Four Screenplays of Ingmar Bergman*. New York: Scribner, 1966.

Bernard, Michael L. *Criteria for Optimal Web Design (Designing for Usability)*. Wichita, KS: Wichita State University, 2003.

Bernard, Michael L., and Mills, Melissa. *Which Fonts Do Children Prefer to Read Online?* Wichita, KS: Wichita State University, 2001.

Black, Alistair, and Rankin, Carolynn. "The History of Children's Library Design: Continuities and Discontinuities." Paper presented at the conference of the International Federation of Library Associations (IFLA). Milan, Italy, August 2009.

Blair, Betty. "Alphabet & Language in Transition." *Azerbaijan International* 8.1 (Spring 2000): 10–12. Available from http://azer.com/aiweb/categories/magazine/81_folder/81_articles/81_editorial.html.

Bloom, Harold, ed. *Stories and Poems for Extremely Intelligent Children of All Ages*. New York: Scribner, 2001.

Blowers, Helene, and Bryan, Robin. *Weaving a Library Web: A Guide to Developing Children's Websites*. Chicago: American Library Association, 2004.

BrainyQuote. http://www.brainyquote.com/quotes/quotes/h/haroldwils104500.html.

Cook, Sherry J., Parker, R. Stephen, and Pettijohn, Charles E. "The Public Library: An Early Teen's Perspective." *Public Libraries* 44.3 (2005): 157–61.

Cooper, H., Nye, B., Charlton, D., Lindsay, J., and Greathouse, S. "Effects of Summer Vacation on Achievement Test Scores: A Narrative and Meta-Analytic Review." *Review of Educational Research* 66 (1996): 227–68.

Cooper, Linda Z. "Developmentally Appropriate Digital Environments for Young Children." *Library Trends* 54.2 (2005): 286–302.

Cordes, Sean. "Broad Horizons: The Role of Multimodal Literacy in 21st Century Instruction." Paper presented at the conference of the International Federation of Library Associations (IFLA). Milan, Italy, August 2009.

Coulmas, Florian. *The Writing Systems of the World*. Oxford: Basil Blackwell, 1989.

Crittendon, Robert. *The New Manager's Starter Kit: Essential Tools for Doing the Job Right*. New York: American Management Association, 2002.

DeLoache, J. S. "Mindful of Symbols." *Scientific American* (August 2005): 60–65.

DeLoache, J. S., Pierroutsakos, Sophia L., Uttal, David H., Rosengren, Karl S., and Gottlieb, Alma. "Grasping the Nature of Pictures." *Psychological Science* 9.3 (1998): 205–10.

Donohue, T. R., Henke, L. L., and Donohue, W. A. "Do Kids Know What TV Commercials Intend?" *Journal of Advertising Research* 20 (1980): 51–56.

Dowd, Nancy, Evangeliste, Mary, and Silberman, Jonathan. *Bite-Sized Marketing: Realistic Solutions for the Overworked Librarian*. Chicago: American Library Association, 2010.

Dresang, Eliza. "The Information-Seeking Behavior of Youth in the Digital Environment." *Library Trends* 54.2 (2005): 178–96.

Dresang, Eliza T. *Radical Change: Books for Youth in a Digital Age*. New York: Wilson, 1999.

Drotner, Kirsten. "Children's Media Culture: A Key to Libraries of the Future?" Paper presented at the conference of the International Federation of Library Associations (IFLA). Milan, Italy, August 2009.

Durgunoglu, Aydin Yucesan, and Verhoeven, Ludo, eds. *Literacy Development in a Multilingual Context*. Mahwah, NJ: Lawrence Erlbaum, 1998.

Eisenberg, Michael B., Lowe, Carrie A., and Spitzer, Kathleen L. *Information Literacy: Essential Skills for the Information Age*. 2nd ed. Westport, CT: Libraries Unlimited, 2004.

Elley, Warwick B. "International and Comparative Assessment of Literacy." *Literacy: An International Handbook*. Ed. Daniel A. Wagner, 1999. 210–16.

Ethnologue Languages of the World. Available from http://www.ethnologue.com/ethno_docs/distribution.asp?by=size.

Fasick, Adele. "Is Literacy for All an Achievable Goal?" *The New Review of Children's Literature and Librarianship* 6 (2000): 37–51.

Fasick, Adele. "Weston Woods Films as Interpretations of Literature." *Children's Literature Association Quarterly* (Fall 1982): 20–22.

Fasick, Adele M., and Holt, Leslie E. *Managing Children's Services in the Public Library*. 3rd ed. Westport, CT: Libraries Unlimited, 2008.

Feinberg, Sandra, and Keller, James R. *Designing Space for Children and Teens in Libraries and Public Places*. Chicago: American Library Association, 2010.

Ferreiro, Emilia. *Past and Present of the Verbs to Read and to Write: Essays on Literacy*. Trans. Mark Fried. Toronto: Douglas & McIntyre, 2000.

Flippo, Rona F. "The Development of Social Skills, Reading, and Literacy Motivation of Pre-School and Kindergarten Children: A Good Fit?" *Journal of Reading Education* 33.2 (2008): 5–10.

Gambrell, Linda B. "Reading Literature, Reading Text, Reading the Internet: The Times They Are a' Changing." *The Reading Teacher* 58.6 (2005): 588–91.

Gentile, Douglas A., Oberg, Nancy E., Sherwood, Mary Story, Walsh, David A., and Hogan, Marjorie. "Well Child Visits in the Video Age: Pediatricians and the American Academy of Pediatrics' Guidelines for Children's Media Use." *Pediatrics* 114 (2004): 1235–41.

Gladwell, Malcolm. *Outliers: The Story of Success*. New York: Little Brown, 2008.

Graff, Harvey J. *The Labyrinths of Literacy: Reflections on Literacy Past and Present.* Rev. and expanded ed. Pittsburgh: University of Pittsburgh Press, 1995.

Healy, Jane M. *Your Child's Growing Mind: Brain Development and Learning from Birth to Adolescence.* 3rd ed. New York: Broadway Books, 2004.

Heller, Robert. *Motivating People.* Essential Managers. Ed. Jane Simmonds. New York: DK Publishing, 1998.

Hogenson, D. L. "Reading Failure and Juvenile Delinquency." *Annals of Dyslexia* 24.1 (1974): 164–69.

Ito, Mizuko. *Living and Learning with New Media: Summary of Findings from the Digital Youth Project.* Cambridge, MA: MIT Press, 2009.

Jackson, Sidney L., Herling, Elinor B., and Josey, E. J. *A Century of Service: Librarianship in the United States and Canada.* Chicago: American Library Association, 1976.

Jaeger, P. T., Bertot, J. C., and McClure, C. R. "The Effects of the Children's Internet Protection Act (CIPA) in Public Libraries and Its Implications for Research: A Statistical, Policy, and Legal Analysis." *Jr. American Society for Information Science* 55.13 (2004): 1131–39.

Jurkowski, Odin. "Schools of Thought: What to Include on Your School Library Web Site." *Children and Libraries* 3.1 (2005): 24–29.

Lehr, Dolores. *Technical and Professional Communication: Integrating Text and Visuals.* Newburyport, MA: Focus Publishing, 2009.

Leigh, Robert D. *The Public Library in the United States.* New York: Columbia University Press, 1950.

Leighton, H. Vernon, Jackson, Joe, Sullivan, Kathryn, and Dennison, Russell F. "Web Page Design and Successful Use: A Focus Group Study." *Internet Reference Services Quarterly* 8.3 (2003): 17–27.

Lunden, Tone. "The Red Thread—New Central Library in Hjoerring, Denmark." Paper presented at the conference of the International Federation of Library Associations (IFLA). Milan, Italy, August 2009.

MacArthur Foundation. *Exploring Digital Media & Learning.* Chicago: MacArthur Foundation, 2009.

Maddox, Brian. "What Good Is Literacy? Insights and Implications of the Capabilities Approach." *Journal of Human Development* 9.2 (2008): 185–206.

Magid, Larry, and Collier, Anne. *MySpace Unraveled: A Parent's Guide to Teen Social Networking from the Directors of Blogsafety.Com.* Berkeley, CA: Peachpit Press, 2007.

Maness, J. "Library 2.0 Theory: Web 2.0 and Its Implications for Libraries." *Webology* 3.2 (2006): Article 25.

Manguel, Alberto. *A History of Reading.* New York: Penguin, 1996.

Margrain, Valerie G. "Case Studies of Precocious Readers: Self-Regulated and Spontaneous Literacy Achievement." *International Society for the Study of Behaviour and Development.* Melbourne, Australia, 2006.

Mathews, Caroline. "The Growing Tendency to Over-Emphasize the Children's Side." *Library Journal* (1908): 135–38.

McFedries, Paul. *Twitter: Tips, Tricks, and Tweets.* 2nd ed. Indianapolis, IN: Wiley, 2010.

Media and Communications in Australian Families 2007: Report of the Media and Society Research Project. Melbourne: Australian Communications and Media Authority, 2007. Available from http://www.acma.gov.au/webwr/_assets/main/lib101058/media_and_society_report_2007.pdf.

Mpe, Phaswane. "Language Policy and African Language Publishing in South Africa." *Bellagio Publishing Newsletter* 25 (1999).

Mulindwa, Gertrude. "After Literacy, What Next? The Challenge of Sustaining a Literate Environment in Botswana." Paper presented at the conference of the International Federation of Library Associations, Section on Reading. Workshop 17. Jerusalem, August, 2000.

Multnomah County Public Library. *Acceptable Use of the Internet and Library Public Computers*. March 17, 2005. http://www.multcolib.org/about/pol-internet.html.

Multnomah County Public Libraries. Book Babies. http://www.multcolib.org/events/storytime.html#babies. Accessed October 23, 2010.

Nazarov, Muzghan. "Library-Based Programs to Promote Literacy: Do They Exist in Azerbaijan?" International Federation of Library Associations, Section on Reading. Workshop 17. Jerusalem, 2000.

Nielsen, Jakob. *Alertbox*. 2002. http://www.useit.com/alertbox/children.html.

Nielsen, Jakob. *Top Ten Mistakes in Web Design*. 2007. http://www.useit.com/alertbox/9605.html.

Onal, H. Inci. "Designing Tomorrow's Libraries with Children's Views." Paper presented at the conference of the International Federation of Library Associations (IFLA). Milan, Italy, August 2009.

Palfrey, John, and Gasser, Urs. *Born Digital: Understanding the First Generation of Digital Natives*. New York: Basic Books, 2008.

Peck, Penny. *Crash Course in Children's Services*. Littleton, CO: Libraries Unlimited, 2006.

Pogue, David. "Apps We Wish We Had." *New York Times*, July 14, 2010. http://www.nytimes.com/2010/07/15/technology/personaltech/15pogue.html.

Rattlesnake Roundup. YouTube. Available at http://www.youtube.com/watch?v=VkiA4 Hhrjuo.

"Reading on the Rise: A New Chapter in American Literacy." Ed. National Endowment for the Arts, 2008.

Rideout, Victoria J., Foehr, Ulla G., and Roberts, Donald F. *Generation M(2): Media in the Lives of 8- to 18-Year-Olds: A Kaiser Family Foundation Study*. 2010. Available from www.kff.org.

Rideout, Victoria J., Vandewater, Elizabeth A., and Wartella, Ellen A. *Zero to Six: Electronic Media in the Lives of Infants, Toddlers and Preschoolers*. Kaiser Family Foundation, 2003. Available from www.kff.org.

Rogers, Henry. *Writing Systems: A Linguistic Approach*. Malden, MA: Blackwell, 2005.

Roman, Susan, Carran, Deborah T., and Fiore, Carole D. *The Dominican Study: Public Library Summer Reading Programs Close the Reading Gap*. River Forest, IL: Dominican University, 2010.

Room for Debate Blog. *New York Times*, February 10, 2010. Available from http://roomfordebate.blogs.nytimes.com/2010/02/10/do-school-libraries-need-books/?emc=eta1.

Seiter, Ellen. *Internet Playground: Children's Access, Entertainment and Mis-Education*. New York: Peter Lang, 2005.

Sen, A. K. "Reflections on Literacy." *Literacy as Freedom*. Ed. C. Robinson. Paris: UNESCO, 2003. 21–30.

Smith, Betty. *A Tree Grows in Brooklyn*. Cutchogue, NY: Buccaneer Books, 1943.

Stephens, Michael. *Web 2.0 & Libraries: Best Practices for Social Software*. Chicago: ALA TechSource, 2006.

Stocks, Elliot Jay. *Sexy Web Design*. Victoria, Australia: Sitepoint, 2009.

Tuccillo, Diane. *Library Teen Advisory Groups*. Lanham, MD: VOYA Books, 2005.

UNESCO. 2011. *Literacy*. Available from http://www.unesco.org/en/literacy.

UNESCO. *Education for All: Literacy for Life*. Paris: UNESCO, 2005.

UNESCO. *The Plurality of Literacy and Its Implications for Policies and Programmes*. Paris: UNESCO, 2004.

Vandewater, Elizabeth A., Rideout, Victoria J., Wartella, Ellen A., Huang, Xuan, Lee, June H., and Shim, Mi-suk Shim. "Digital Childhood Electronic Media and Technology Use among Infants, Toddlers, and Preschoolers." *Pediatrics* 119.5 (2007): 1006–15.

Varvel, Virgil E. Jr., and Lei, Xinrong. "Characteristics and Trends in the Public Library Data Service 2008 Report." *Public Libraries* 48.2 (2009): 6–12.

Wagner, Daniel A., and Stites, Regie. "Literacy Skill Retention." *Literacy: An International Handbook.* Ed. Daniel Wagner. Boulder, CO: Westview Press, 1999. 199–202.

Walter, Virginia. *Children and Libraries: Getting It Right.* Chicago: American Library Association, 2001.

Walter, Virginia. *Output Measures for Public Library Service to Children: A Manual of Standardized Procedures.* Chicago, IL: American Library Association, 1992.

Weber, Sandra, and Dixon, Shanly. *Growing Up Online: Young People and Digital Technologies.* New York: Palgrave Macmillan, 2007.

Wertham, Frederic. *Seduction of the Innocent.* New York: Rinehart, 1954.

West, James A., and West, Margaret L. *Using Wikis for Online Collaboration: The Power of the Read-Write Web.* San Francisco, CA: Jossey-Bass, 2009.

Wibbels, Andy. *Blog Wild! A Guide for Small Business Blogging.* New York: Penguin, 2006.

Wolf, Maryanne. *Proust and the Squid: The Story and Science of the Reading Brain.* New York: Harper, 2007.

Xiaomei, Cai, and Zhao Xiaoquan. "Click Here, Kids!" *Journal of Children & Media* 4.2 (2009): 135–54.

Zevenbergen, Robyn, and Logan, Helen. "Computer Use by Preschool Children: Rethinking Practice as Digital Natives Come to Preschool." *Australian Journal of Early Childhood* 33.1 (2008).

INDEX

ABOUT THE AUTHOR

ADELE M. FASICK is professor emerita of the Faculty of Information Studies, University of Toronto, and teaches at San Jose State University. Dr. Fasick is the author of *Child View: Evaluating and Reviewing Material for Children* (with Claire England) and *Managing Children's Services in Public Libraries*, 3rd ed. (with Leslie Holt). She has been active in national and international library associations.